TENBY TO CELTIC MANOR
A History of Golf in Wales

Tenby to Celtic Manor
A History of Golf in Wales

Byron Kalies

First published in 2010

© Byron Kalies

© Gwasg Carreg Gwalch 2010

Published with the financial support
of the Welsh Books Council

ISBN: 978-1-84524-304-6

Cover design: Sion Ilar

Published by Gwasg Carreg Gwalch,
12 Iard yr Orsaf, Llanrwst, Wales LL26 0EH
tel: 01492 624031
fax: 01492 641502
email: books@carreg-gwalch.com
website: www.carreg-gwalch.com

Contents

Acknowledgements

This book is a selective trawl through the history of Golf in Wales to the present day. I've tried to get a mix of large Clubs and small Clubs, members' Clubs and owners' Clubs, urban Clubs and rural Clubs. This is a snapshot of golf as I saw it and heard it in the summer of 2009 in Wales.

Many thanks are due for the help, support and patience I've had from the Golf Club managers, secretaries, captains, members, Club historians and professionals across Wales. Special thanks to the people who have patiently hunted for papers in the backs of cupboards, answered my queries, sent me notes, records, books and photos.

Particular apologies to the club officials who don't find their Club in this book. In attempting to give the widest range of Clubs in Wales I've had to be incredibly selective – sorry.

Introduction

*Golf was one of the fastest growing recreational sports
in Britain before 1914.*

Wray Vamplew,
historian of sports economics

The Ryder Cup

In 1926 a group of American professionals arrived in England
to play in the Open Golf Championship at Wentworth.
With a few days on their hands while they waited for the
Open to begin they competed against a team of British
professionals, but lost 13½ points to 1½ points.

Samuel Ryder, a wealthy Englishman, watched the
competition, and agreed to provide a trophy to encourage
the matches to be played on a regular basis.

The inaugural Ryder Cup matches were played the
following year at Worcester Country Club in Massachusetts,
and thereafter every two years, with the venue alternating
between England and America. In 1973 the Cup was played
for in Scotland for the first time, at Muirfield, and in 1979,
after a period of American supremacy, it was decided to
include European players in the competition. Since then the
contest have been close, and the score remains Europe 7
wins, America 7 wins, and one tied match.

The Ryder Cup remains one of the few great sporting
competitions that is played for no prize money.

October 2010 will see the Ryder Cup held in Wales, for
the first time ever. The Ryder Cup is a three-day
competition between teams representing Europe and the
USA. It is the third biggest sporting occasion on earth,
surpassed only by the Olympic Games and the football
World Cup. It is watched by billions of people across the
world. In 2010 the matches will be played on the Celtic

Manor Resort's new 'Twenty Ten' course in Newport, Wales: the first golf course specifically designed to host the biennial event.

But golf in Wales does not begin and end with the 2010 Ryder Cup. The Ryder Cup will obviously be fantastic for Wales, for tourism, for the economy, but for golf itself the hope is that it will bring world recognition that Wales is a great place to play golf. Although there are fewer than 200 Golf Clubs in Wales, compared with over 7,000 in the rest of the UK, the diversity and beauty of the courses is superb. It is hoped that more people will realise that golf in Wales can be a rich and varied experience, every bit as exciting as golf in Scotland or Ireland.

Origins of golf

The last fifty years of the Victorian era were a time of dramatic change for Wales. The population virtually doubled between 1851 and 1901. In 1851, 35 per cent of the population of Wales earned their living in agriculture. By the early twentieth century this was down to 10 per cent. In 1850 almost all elected MPs were members of the land-owning classes; by 1914 only three of the thirty-four MPs representing Welsh constituencies were part of the landed gentry. The rôle of women was about to change, as was the power of the Church.

Golf, and sport in general, reflected the changing times. In 1876 the Football Association was formed in Wales. In 1881 the Welsh Rugby Union was formed. In 1888 Glamorgan County Cricket Club was founded. In 1895 the Welsh Golfing Union was formed with a meeting of seven existing Clubs: Tenby, Porthcawl, Swansea Bay, Glamorganshire, Caernarvonshire, Borth-Ynylas, Aberdovey and Merionethshire.

The WGU might have been a new organisation, but golf

was not a new sport. There are reports of golf being played in Scotland as early as the twelfth century. with shepherds knocking balls into holes with sticks (or, knocking chuckies into hawls with crummocks). Eight hundred years later the chuckies may well now be Titleist Pro V1 and your 'relief' crummock could have a polymer cord hybrid black grip. Yet essentially it's the same game: your task is to get the pebble into the rabbit hole with the least number of cloots.

In 1744 the first Golf Club was formed, The Gentlemen Golfers of Edinburgh. In 1754 The Royal and Ancient Golf Club of St Andrews was founded. Over the two and a half centuries it has been in existence it has evolved and now has a separate entity, the 'R&A', set up as golf's governing body. The R&A decides (with the United States Golf Association) all golf rule changes throughout the World.

In 1864 the first English club was formed, the North Devon Club at Westwood Ho!.

Origins of golf in Wales
The largest impact on the game in Wales was the arrival of the railways. Between 1860 and 1900 railway-building expanded phenomenally, reaching almost every part of Wales. They were used to transport coal, iron ore, goods, food and people. The arrival of the railway affected every part of Welsh life. The effect on the industrial valleys was overwhelming, but the effect on rural area and coastal towns was also remarkable. Various Acts of Parliament gave benefits to workers in terms of holidays for the middle and working classes. Three seaside towns in particular were developed as holiday centres: Aberystwyth, Swansea and Tenby. These resorts and other areas in north Wales (such as Pwllheli, Llandudno, Rhyl) and other tourist towns such as Llandrindod Wells, Builth Wells (which were on routes to seaside resorts) needed attractions for the visitors,

something to attract people to *their* particular town. Golf was one of those attractions. Golf courses and towns in the Victorian age met the needs of affluent visitors. These visitors would stay in fashionable hotels, play golf in the finest resorts, on the finest courses. Over a century later, not a lot has changed.

For the less affluent visitors to Wales there were other attractions at resorts; donkey rides, Punch and Judy shows, museums, boat trips, theatres and cinemas, and swimming pools. And if the town wasn't large enough or wealthy enough to build a full golf course, there was usually 'crazy golf' and small pitch-and-putt courses.

The tourist industry, although a large part of the boom in golf, wasn't the only reason golf was played in Wales. The other, perhaps more important, driving force behind setting up a golf Club was more traditional, with like-minded business people developing a Club very much for themselves. This was the mark of elitism in some towns. There were waiting lists to join the clubs. There was a selection process. To all intents and purposes it was an exclusive Gentleman's Club. This exclusivity wasn't only for the extremely well-off or royalty – it operated at a variety of levels. In the valleys of south-east Wales the elitism was the same as for some of the richer clubs such as Cardiff, Newport and Porthcawl. Newcomers had to be vetted and ensured they were the 'right sort'. The people running golf courses and playing golf in the first half of golf's history in Wales have been stereotyped, rather unfairly, as 'the silly-trousered brigade'. This alludes to the dress code and attire golfers have traditionally had to endure. Whilst there was an element of 'us and them', it often belied a great deal of hard work and finance that went into creating and maintaining golf clubs, especially in the financially difficult years between the wars.

Changes

Throughout the twentieth century golf itself changed considerably with the increased rate of change of technology. In basic terms the equipment and the courses were greatly improved. In 1919 the course at Southerndown, for example, needed to be shortened and made easier as the rounds were taking an average of five hours!

At the start of the century golf clubs were still made from hard wood, and had wooden shafts. As the century progressed things changed slowly. After the Second World War 'irons' were introduced. They were made initially of iron, then later, steel. 'Woods' were the clubs that had a fatter head and hit the ball further than irons, and their heads were made, unsurprisingly, of wood. Then there was a great deal of development into synthetic and composite materials. In 1973 graphite shafts were introduced. Then a very strange term entered golf – 'metal woods'. These were clubs with the same shape as traditional woods, but the heads were made of metal and proved more resilient and hit the ball further. These were followed by 'woods' with bigger heads, and 'woods' made with all sorts of metals, including aluminium, titanium or even scandium.

Other technological and social changes also helped the development of golf. From the 1960s people could see golf on the television. There were players the public could admire and hope to emulate. The era of heroes such as Jack Niklaus, Gary Player and Arnold Palmer influenced many people to have a go at golf themselves. Interestingly the same sort of pattern is repeating itself today with an increased interest in golf – especially youngsters. From the late 1990s the new symbol of golf was Tiger Woods, who popularised golf in a way no-one else ever has.

The 'boom years' were great for golf in Wales. Demand outstripped resources and the 1960s and 1970s were a time when farmers and others decided that golf could be the future for them. More and more Golf Clubs were opened. Fields were converted to driving ranges, farms were changed into golf courses and the number of people playing golf increased rapidly.

Unfortunately the boom of the past thirty years has waned somewhat. The credit crunch has begun to affect all aspects of life and many Golf Clubs are facing real difficulties. Golf Clubs had, to some extent, become quite lazy and complacent. Many clubs had full memberships and long waiting lists of potential members. If costs increased then the Club simply increased the fees; some members complained, but not too much. There were not enough other Clubs for them to move to.

However, as costs began to rise rapidly over the past decade or so and more Clubs opened, the numbers of people on waiting lists began to diminish. Soon many Golf Clubs began to feel the strain. A number of Clubs have transformed themselves after realising that Clubs are a commodity, and they have began to act as a business. For other Clubs the past decade, and in particular the past year or so, have been extremely difficult. But all Clubs now seem to be aware of the dangers and are working incredibly hard to keep golf alive. Golf Clubs have realised their clubhouses are good sources of income and have began marketing them and hiring them out for weddings, conferences, etc. Clubs are working with other clubs in business 'clusters' designed to give golfers a great deal playing a number of courses in the area – there are clusters in central Wales, south-west Wales and north-east Wales.

Values
Socially, Golf Clubs have, in general, realised that this is the twenty-first century and that Victorian values are a thing of

the past. The early disputes in Golf Clubs revolved around playing golf on the Sabbath and allowing drinking to take place in the club house. Today this all seems a little silly and unbelievable for many people, yet the same battle has had to be fought concerning the roles of women and youngsters. Most Clubs say that this discrimination is a thing of the past, yet females and juniors are often given very different treatment – they have special times set aside for them to play, they are not allowed to sit on all committees, they are not allowed to enter competitions.

More and more clubs have had to realise that excluding women and youngsters is not just morally wrong but financially ridiculous. Today many clubs are actively encouraging groups that were often previously excluded.

Golf's future
In the early days the needs of the Club members were paramount, and Clubs traditionally tended to discourage visits by golfers from other Clubs. But there has always been a need to balance the needs of the Club's own members and the financial needs of the Club, and today, as costs rise and rise, Clubs are reaching out to golfers from other clubs, other countries and even golfers not attached to any Club.

It has been estimated that 70 per cent of golfers do not belong to a Club. This large group, usually part of a company, a village or a pub, was frequently shunned in the past, so they would get together and form a 'Golf Society'. They would organise a day out at a Golf Club which would consist of golf and meals in a reasonably-priced package. However, the past twenty or thirty years has seen the rise and the decline of these societies. Initially Clubs were reluctant to accept Societies for fear of upsetting the members, who wanted to play their course with no restrictions. Then the Clubs embraced these societies as this formed a good part of their finances for the year. Even members could see the sense of this.

Now golfers have become more sophisticated and want more than a day out. They want a mini-break with golf at a number of courses over two or three days. These have been incredibly popular in Scotland and Ireland. Welsh Clubs have began to realise that this is a good opportunity to get some much-needed money into the Clubs, and clusters of Clubs have started to work together to develop these activities and provide more tailored packages for golfers.

This is one area where Clubs are changing and working more effectively. There are other initiatives taking place where Clubs encourage juniors and women to try golf before they join a Golf Club. More and more Welsh Clubs are beginning to strip away the prejudices and barriers people have about playing golf.

This book is a history of Golf Clubs in Wales, Clubs of all varieties. The main feature of Welsh golf over the century and a quarter of its life has been resilience, the sense of not giving in. This seems to be as true today as it has been in the past. Every Club has its unique story of the hard times it has had to go through, and is going through now. I feel hopeful, though, that this resilience will see most of the Clubs through the difficult times. Perhaps the best example for me was the story of the smallest Club I visited, Rhosgoch. The Club had collapsed; it was the sheer determination of the members that revived it and has kept it going for a decade, and will continue to keep it going. The Club itself says it is 'In the community, owned and run by the community, for the community'.

Rural Rhosgoch and luxurious Celtic Manor, the venue for the 2010 Ryder Cup competition, are at opposite ends of the Golf Club scale, but they are essentially the same, as are the other 174 golf courses in Wales. They have a history, a passion for golf, and a story. The members of these diverse clubs, and all the clubs in Wales have a common purpose – to play golf. Over the years this seemingly uncomplicated aim has sometimes proved not quite as straightforward as it might have been. This book tells some of these stories.

Chapter 1

TENBY
Founded 1888

Tenby is a bustling town on the southwest coast of Wales
with an unusually high concentration of pubs.

www.worldgolf.com

Tenby, *Dinbych-y-Pysgod* ('little fort of the fish') in Welsh, has existed for a long time. It lies on the coast of southern Pembrokeshire, 27 miles west of Carmarthen. The first mention of the town was in a ninth-century bardic poem. It grew in the twelfth century. The Norman castle was built to keep out the Welsh. In the fourteenth, fifteenth and sixteenth centuries it was a major port. After this, however, the town slept until the railways woke it.

By the early nineteenth century Tenby had become a pretty, historical town with a busy fishing community. Victorians were keen on health, and 'taking the waters' was a great Victorian passion. The growth of the town and the tourism went hand in hand, and the trickle of tourists in the first half of the nineteenth century became a flood as the railway arrived at Tenby in 1863. By 1888 it was a tourist-driven town. Amongst the visitors to Tenby at this time were novelists Lewis Carroll, Jane Austen, and George Eliot; the artist J. M. W. Turner; and Beatrix Potter, creator of Peter Rabbit and friends.

There were hotel-owners and business-owners in the

town who were keen golfers themselves and eager for something extra to attract their customers to the area. Setting up and developing the Club was a mixture of business and pleasure for them. In Tenby, as in a number of Welsh seaside towns, golf had a dual purpose: as well as the tourism angle, the Club became a focus for local businesspeople to relax, play and meet.

These days Tenby still pulls in the tourists. They come to walk the Pembrokeshire Coastal Path, or to go across to Caldey Island to see the perfume-making monks, and the town itself has an annual Arts Festival. Not too far away is Laugharne, of Dylan Thomas fame. And of course, there is always golf ...

Beginnings

Tenby is believed to be the oldest Golf Club in Wales. It was established after a meeting on 31 September 1888 in the Town Hall, when six people decided to form a Club. The first membership fees were 10/6d per year or 5/- per month (equivalent to £273 or £130 today).

However, there is some evidence that golf had been played at Tenby as early as 1875. A passage in *Laws of Markets and Fairs* published in that year refers to court proceedings being adjourned whilst the court officials took time off to play golf.

The first Club competition was held on 21 October 1888, when thirty-three gentlemen and ladies took part and a Mr. T. A. Rees was the winner with a gross 51, net 41 off a 10 handicap (9 holes).

The Club prospered in the early years. In 1889 there were ninety recorded members. In 1892 there was sufficient money and optimism to employ a groundsman. There is a record in 1911 of comparative wages: whilst the Professional was paid 15/- a week, the green-keeper was paid 35/- per week.

The Club developed in the late Victorian era. A number of improvements were made to the course and exhibition matches are recorded. It was also the time when Tenby played home and away matches with Ashburnham in 1896. This, the oldest surviving Welsh fixture, is still played today.

In 1907 James Braid developed the full eighteen-hole course which was opened at the Easter meeting that same year.

*View from Black Rock of 18th hole and
1st fairway around 1910*

More alterations were made between the war years. It is recorded that part of the course was landmined in 1940.

There have been a number of clubhouses over the years, even one in the town. The current one was opened in 1966 at a cost of £40,000. Over recent years this has been refurbished and extended. It is also one of the most modern-looking clubhouses in Wales.

With the help of partners such as the Ryder Cup Legacy Fund the Club are working hard at improving facilities and attracting more members. The fund will help Tenby Club develop a three-hole short course specifically designed to make golf more accessible and enjoyable for juniors and newcomers to golf. There will also be better practice facilities. This is essential as the Club holds more prestigious tournaments. In 2010 the Club will host the Welsh Amateur Championship and the British Ladies Championship.

With the support of Golf Development Wales the Club Professional, Mark Hawkey, has introduced 'taster sessions' over the past year. At a subsidised cost of around £1 a person over 150 potential new golfers have had the opportunity to try golf out and see if they like it. Following on from this the Club has encouraged more people to join by introducing more flexible membership deals with three-month trial memberships or six-monthly memberships.

So, whilst Tenby is justifiably proud of its heritage and its unique place in Welsh golf history, David Hancock (Secretary) sums up the approach: 'It's about not living in the past, but keeping moving forward.'

Design of the course
One name is inextricably linked with Tenby golf course – James Braid. He was a keen golfer at a young age and won his first tournament at the age of eight. He became a club-maker, and turned professional in 1896, moving to Romford Golf Club. Although he had an excellent long game his putting let him down. In 1900 he switched to an aluminium-headed putter and won five of the next nine Open Championships.

However, it was as a course designer that he felt his great passion. He designed over 200 courses in Britain including Carnoustie, Troon, Prestwick and Ballybunion. He also

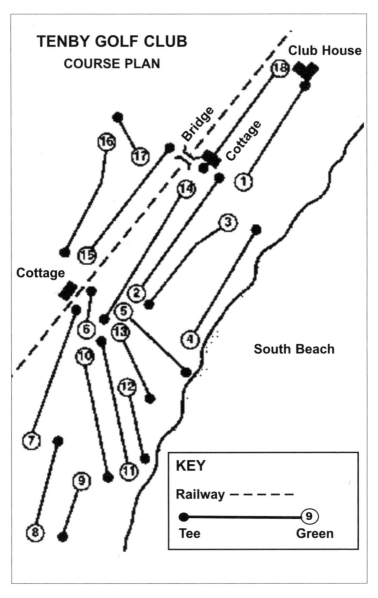

*Simple line drawing of Tenby golf course showing the
traditional 'out and back' course design*

remodelled twenty courses in Wales. He tended to work in the same way on each job: he charged a low fee, communicated his ideas quickly and effectively, and was diplomatic enough to keep the greens committees happy.

James Braid was brought to the Tenby Club early in its existence. In July 1902 he was paid £6 to inspect the course and suggest improvements. Five years later the course had expanded to eighteen holes with more input and advice from James Braid. This new course was opened at Easter in 1907.

In 1927 he was again asked to help with the structure of the course. He made further alterations and suggestions about the layout. There have been minor changes over the years but basically the course is the same as when James Braid finished remodelling it.

The layout is pleasantly old-fashioned. Originally in golf you teed up for the next hole within a few clubs' length of the hole you had just played. At Tenby this tradition is maintained with the tees still situated close to the greens. There are few sand bunkers at Tenby – they were very difficult to maintain in the early days of golf.

One unusual feature of the course is that the holes all have a story behind them. For instance the third is 'Dai Rees' because the famous golfer really liked the hole; 'Monk's Way', the ninth, is a reference to the path the monks would take on their journey from the town to Caldey island; the tenth is called 'James Braid' for obvious reasons.

The players' view

'There are longer courses that are less challenging and shorter courses that are more difficult, but Tenby is fun and difficult.'

– John Hopkins, *Golf Wales*

'Tenby offers fantastic value for money in winter. Expect a truly special golfing outing.'

— *2 FORE 1 Course Factfile*

'The legendary Dai Rees was so enamoured with James Braid's design that the 3rd hole, his favourite, is named after him. Tenby is a classic links experience.'

— *Golf World*

'The gently rolling James Braid links offer a string of classy, short holes, while the greens were splendidly true and faster than most in midseason.'

— *Today's Golfer*

'This most traditional archetypal links is the oldest course in Wales and those who find their way to Pembrokeshire, in the south west of the Principality, will be richly rewarded. Every round at Tenby is a new experience but what can be guaranteed is a warm welcome at a club that seems to appreciate the lengths to which many of its visitors go to.'

— *National Club Golf*

'Tenby boasts great links terrain filled with excellent views of the coast and plenty of quirks. It's reminiscent of an unrefined Prestwick in a lot of ways: a historic, nineteenth-century pedigree and an imaginative routing with lots of thick rough.'

— *World Golf.com*

'Tenby was my favourite course in Wales. The blind shots didn't seem overwhelming and the drama of high dunes and deep hollows more than compensated for this lack of visibility. The greens, true, fast, and always undulating, were the best we'd seen in Wales.'

— Robert Kroeger, *The Links of Wales*

Details

Tenby Golf Club
The Burrows
Tenby
SA70 7NP

01834 842978
Location: From Tenby town take Station Road from the A4139
Type of course: links
Par: 71
Course yardage: 6,224

website: www.tenbygolf.co.uk

Chapter 2

ROYAL PORTHCAWL
Founded 1892

*I loved Porthcawl as a nipper, half our village would be there
for Miners' Holiday. Caravan at Trecco Bay, mini-golf,
family outings to the Jolly Sailor pub, the dodgy old funfair.*

'Belushi', www.urban75.net blog

Porthcawl is situated 30 miles west of Cardiff and 22 miles
east of Swansea. It is set on the South Wales coast
overlooking the Bristol Channel, and is one of Wales' most
enduring holiday resorts. There are a number of beaches
fringing the town. It has evolved into a seaside town since
the Victorian era. It was a favourite venue for miners from
the south Wales valleys for many years during 'Miners'
Fortnight' (the two-week holiday from work given to
miners) filling every caravan and guesthouse in the town.
There is currently a lot of refurbishment going on in the
town and there are plans to bring visitors back to Porthcawl
after they were lured away by cheap Spanish 'Costas'
holidays in the 1960s. The striking Grand Pavilion, built of
ferrocrete and opened in 1932, is still the place for
entertainments and cinema.

Beginnings
Undoubtedly the most prestigious Golf Club in Wales is
Royal Porthcawl. The Club originated when a group of

Cardiff businessmen met to form a Golf Club in 1891. Many of these men were involved in the export of coal and in various other shipping activities. It had been an extremely fruitful period for them: many had made their fortunes over the preceding decades. The coal from the valleys had been plentiful and very much in demand and many coal and rail entrepreneurs and owners had acquired a great deal of wealth. Cardiff in particular was the place to be, in terms of finance and opportunity. In 1880 72 per cent of coal exported from Britain came from Wales and Cardiff was recognised as the most important coal port in the world. To meet the increasing demands docks were being built to the immediate west of Cardiff at Barry. Cardiff in 1901 had increased its population sevenfold from 1851 and the city was the place where many of the wealthy merchants of south Wales and southern England eventually settled.

In this period where the workers had their rugby clubs, the owners were looking for their own sport. The Golf Club at Porthcawl was set up by a number of wealthy businessmen and built on the traditional Victorian values described by author of *A Dictionary of Victorian Britain*, Lee Jackson, in an article on *www.bbc.co.uk* as 'positive, moralistic, upstanding'.

On 13 November 1891 the first meeting took place to decide on rules and a venue. As many of the founder members made their living through exporting coal from Cardiff and Barry Docks they would have been familiar with the coast around these towns. They unsurprisingly settled on Porthcawl, an eighteenth-century coal-exporting centre and a town just beginning to become popular as a tourist resort.

Early lists of members read like a *Who's Who* of the rich of Cardiff and the Vale of Glamorgan. On the register of members from 1895 are a number of ministers, solicitors,

army and navy officers, doctors, professors, and even Lord
Tredegar of Tredegar Park, Newport. The Club seems very
much aware of what a special position it has, and the whole
place has developed an atmosphere of exclusivity or elitism
that goes with being confident that Royal Porthcawl is the
best. The staff are polite, courteous and a little deferential.
There is a sense of awe when you enter the changing rooms,
almost that of walking backwards into a Victorian era.
There's a feeling of 'class' about the place. It seems to be
something that goes with the Club, part of the people, part
of the buildings. The rest home next to the clubhouse is the
place where Florence Nightingale worked; the bars and
changing rooms are full of photographs of legends who have
walked the corridors of the Club. John Hopkins writes of the
members at Royal Porthcawl:

> For well over one century they have hung their jackets on
> hooks that look as though they are over one hundred
> years old, sat on benches that have served thousands of
> golfers down the years and noted the memorabilia that
> surrounds them – the photographs of the Club captains
> for example, the portrait of Edward VIII, the Prince of
> Wales, who would become a patron of the Club.
>
> *Golf Wales*, Graffeg, 2007

It is something that sets them apart from most other Welsh
Golf Clubs. It may be a possible problem in the future. As
golf becomes a more and more democratic and populist
game will Royal Porthcawl be able to survive charging over
£100 a round and recruiting new members by invitation
only? I suspect the answer will be 'yes'. Modern business
theory would say that although 99 per cent of businesses
survive by being 'fit': lean, dynamic and flexible, there is still
the 1 per cent – Ferrari, Harley-Davidson, BMW, Gibson

Les Paul, St. Andrews and Royal Porthcawl – that survive by being 'sexy': unique, timeless, prestigious.

The fact that the Club hasn't got the necessary infrastructure, transport systems, space, hospitality accommodation etc. to hold major golfing tournaments seems a double-edged sword. No doubt some are pleased the Club can resist the change. Others, however, feel differently. Leo McMahon, writing in *Royal Porthcawl 1891–1991*, sums it up:

> Regrettably shamefully, short-sightedly or mercifully, depending on one's viewpoint, Royal Porthcawl has not had these ingredients (the infrastructure) in measure enough to attract much in the way of professional golf in recent years, while in years gone by there was probably little fire in Members' bellies to pay much heed to professional golf.

It is a special Club. It is rated the top course in Wales, and in the top 100 golf courses in the world by the prestigious *Top 100 Golf Courses in the World*. It consistently figures in the top courses to play by most magazines and professionals. It has hosted many leading amateur and professional tournaments, including the Walker Cup, the Amateur Championship (six times) Curtis Cup, European Team Championship, the Home Internationals (eight times), the Ladies British Open Amateur, Dunlop Masters, the Penfold and the Coral Classic. It's the course where Tiger Woods lost his singles in the 1995 Walker Cup to Gary Wolstenholme and the USA team lost 14–10 to Great Britain and Ireland.

'Royal' Porthcawl

The Lord Mayor of Cardiff received the invitation that it was the intention of His Majesty to confer the title Royal on the Porthcawl Golf Club. This is the result of efforts which have been made for months past by Mr Wyndham Jenkins, captain of the Club, to secure Royal recognition of the institution.

South Wales Daily News, 1 April 1909

How the 'Royal' came about is quite a mystery. The documentation that exists shows that the Club had petitioned before, but the reply from the Home Secretary of the time, Herbert Gladstone, indicated that this was not likely to happen: 'Having regard to the precedents which govern such grants, after careful consideration I am unable to advise His Majesty to grant the desired privilege.'

However, just six months later a letter arrived, again from Gladstone, this time informing the Club that 'After enquiry and consideration I have felt able to recommend the King to permit the Club to use the title 'Royal' and that His Majesty has been pleased to approve the recommendation.'

It was not until 1932 that a member of the royal family played a round of golf at Royal Porthcawl. In that year HRH Edward, Prince of Wales, played for the Household Brigade against The Erratics at The Berkshire. He played there again that same year: on 10 December he played a fourball with Selwyn Martin, Captain at the time, against Robert Orr and John Duncan. Legend has it that the match was played with all players speaking Spanish as the Prince was due to leave for Argentina the following day and needed the practice. It was exactly four years before his abdication.

The magnificent portrait of the Prince by Hal Ludlow was painted at this time and has hung in the clubhouse ever since.

Culture

In the excellent centenary book, *Royal Porthcawl 1891–1991*, edited by Leo McMahon, there are a number of extracts which give a flavour of the Club and the attitude of the members:

> Over the years it was decided to allow men into the Ladies' room after 6.00 p.m. and on weekend afternoons. However, this is not encouraged and very few gentlemen visit.

> In 1969 it was decided trouser suits would not be worn in the clubhouse as they might be offensive to the men.

> During the First World War all commanding officers and the officers of the Regiments stationed in the area were made honorary members. This was stopped in 1919.

> In 1943 American troops were stationed in Porthcawl and their officers were made honorary members.

Porthcawl lady golfers. At the start, all ladies' competitions were organised by men

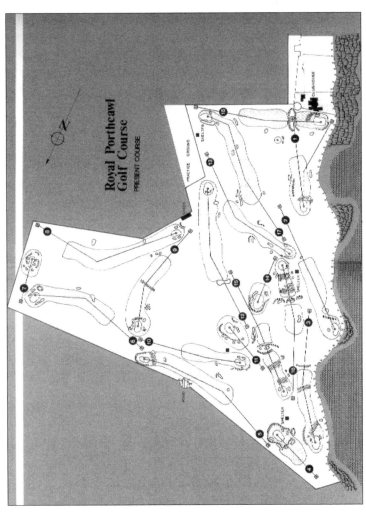

Current golf course plan showing the changing direction of holes, which makes it difficult to establish any rhythm

In the first hundred years of the Golf Club, Royal Porthcawl only employed three golf professionals. The first was J. G. Hutcheson, professional from 1899 to 1951. The Centenary book tells that 'Hutch', as he was known, would go into the bar at the end of the day and ask the steward for the drinks he had been left that day by grateful players. He would have the seven, eight or however many whiskies in a tumbler with a ginger ale. Then he would walk to Porthcawl, and at exactly 8 p.m. enter the barber's shop of "Scoop" Churchill for a shave.

The second Professional was Walter Clifford Gould who served as Assistant then professional on Hutch's death in 1951 until 1979. The third was Graham Poor, who arrived in 1979 from Llanwern Golf Club.

Design of the course

The original nine-hole course was laid out on Locks Common by Charles Gibson, the Professional from the oldest links in England. His Club was Westwood Ho! in Devon (now the Royal North Devon Golf Club), where he started as a clubmaker and Professional in 1888. He was the oldest golf Professional in England at the time of his death in 1932, aged sixty-eight.

A few years later Porthcawl course was extended to eighteen holes. Not long after that the original nine holes were abandoned and the course laid out on land forming part of the Manor of Sker. This is where the course has remained. The layout of the course is designed to test skill, as the holes zig-zag along the coast playing into the wind, then across the wind, then with the wind. Tremendous skill is needed as the players have to keep adjusting to compensate. The greens are fast, undulating and very testing. To complete the test the course is invariably played in a fair amount of wind as there are no high dunes or trees to shield the ball.

In 1933 Tom Simpson was invited to inspect the course. Simpson was an amateur golf course architect who didn't need the money. He was by all accounts a plain speaker, often controversial. Henry Longhurst wrote of him in his obituary: 'His life has been one of unwavering hostility towards government by committees in any shape or form and of ceaseless endeavour to get 'one up' on them.'

Simpson's report declared the course 'The finest piece of natural 'Links Land' that we have seen in the United Kingdom.' He did, however, say it needed further work. The alterations were made at a cost of £1,553.

In 1950 C. K. Potter made some minor changes, as did Donald Steel in 1986.

A character

One of the early presidents of the Club was William James Tatem (1915–1942), who later became Lord Glanely. He was born in Appledore, North Devon and became one of the richest men of the day having founded the Tatem Steam Navigation Company. He became a director of most of the shipping companies operating from Bute Docks, Cardiff which further increased his wealth. He was a racehorse owner, chairman of the University College, Cardiff, High Sheriff of Glamorgan, and by all accounts a buccaneering figure. How he gained his peerage has become the stuff of legends. He allegedly handed over a cheque for £50,000 to the political organiser working for David Lloyd George. The organiser asked Mr. Tatem why the cheque was signed 'Glanely'. Tatem replied; 'Because my name is going to be Lord Glanely, and if it isn't, you won't be able to cash that cheque.' He became Baron in 1916 and in 1918 gained a peerage as the 1st Baron Glanely of St. Fagans.

In 1919 he had two horses entered for the Derby. His favourite, as he told everyone, and the racing favourite was

Dominion. The other, Grand Parade, who he secretly bet on, romped home at 33/1. His horses also won every other classic; 1,000 guineas, 2,000 guineas, Oaks and St. Leger.

Lord Glanely died in a bombing raid on Weston-super-Mare, Somerset in 1942.

The players' view

'The visitors may pass through two bars ... and up to the 1st tee where they will confront a magnificent course that has the true characteristics of a links course and, in addition, the bonus of having the sea being visible from every hole.'

– John Hopkins, *Golf Wales*

On the speed of the greens: 'Putting into bunkers is quite commonplace, and one renowned lady golfer of yesteryear is alleged to have lost her ball putting downhill and downwind on the 5th green.'

– Leo McMahon

'For links of this calibre, it's an unexpected and pleasant surprise – and symbolizes Wales' niche as a destination where the quality of courses supersedes their international reputation.

– Brandon Tucker, senior writer, *www.worldgolf.com*

'So far, Porthcawl is unspoiled, and it is very good. It is a place to go to. Some day it will be exploited to the very utmost, and in these matters one likes to be in at the beginning.'

– Tom Scott, *Golf Illustrated*

'Royal Porthcawl epitomises all that is best about the game, as it once was, even down to a creaking clubhouse that is as unchanging as the magnificent links and unrivalled hospitality.

– Michael Williams, *Daily Telegraph*

Details

Royal Porthcawl Golf Club
Rest Bay
Porthcawl
CF36 3UW

01656 782251

Location: 2 miles/3.2 km from J37 off the M4
Type of course: Championship downland/links
Par: 72
Course yardage: 6,740

website: www.royalporthcawl.com

Chapter 3

MONMOUTH
Founded 1896

Against a background of pastel-painted Georgian prosperity,
the compact market town of Monmouth bustles and thrives.

– Neil Wilson, *Lonely Planet* series – Wales

The town of Monmouth, built on the confluence of the rivers Wye and Monnow, is on the eastern border of Wales 15 miles north of Chepstow. Over the centuries Monmouth has been in and out of Wales as the border has shifted back and forth Over the years there have been struggles and conflicts in this strategic Welsh border town, and it has seen more than its fair share of bloodshed.

There was the battle of Monmouth (*Trefynwy*) in 1233 between the royalist, John of Monmouth and the rebel forces of Richard Marshal, 3rd Earl of Pembroke – the rebels won the day. This battle was held on Vauxhall fields, an early site for the Golf Club.

Henry V of Battle of Agincourt fame was born in Monmouth castle, and Owain Glyndŵr led a rebellion and fought a number of battles in the area.

In 1840 the Chartist protestors John Frost, Zephaniah Williams and William Jones were the last men in Britain sentenced to be hanged, drawn and quartered. This was at the Shire Hall in Monmouth. Their sentence was later commuted to transportation to Australia.

In 1605 James I granted a Charter to the town, which included the phrase that the town 'at all perpetual future times ... be and remain a town and borough of Peace and Quiet, to the example and terror of the wicked and reward of the good'.

Nearby twelfth-century Tintern Abbey certainly has an atmosphere of peace and quiet, and there are spectacular views to be had from Raglan castle, not far away.

Beginnings

With this history it would hardly seem surprising that the Monmouth Club had troubles in its early years. The early years of the Club were a time of great social uncertainty. Admittedly this was less dramatic than previous times of chaos, war and death, but this was nevertheless a time of insecurity for landowners and farm workers in rural Wales, and Monmouth. The town, set in the heart of arable farmland alongside the Wye, was in a typical agricultural area of Wales. At the end of the nineteenth-century inhabitants were dependent on a few wealthy landowners. In the years just around the beginning of the Club there was a transformation of the farming industry. This period was often seen as a time of great prosperity for many in the countryside and a golden age where life was simpler and easier. However, there was also unrest as many wealthy landowners became unsatisfied with the income they received from tenants and put their land on the market. In this area, for instance, the Duke of Beaufort put 7000 hectares of Monmouthshire land up for auction in 1902. Much of this land was bought by tenants, which led to significant changes in society as farmers moved from being workers to being owners. Prices of agricultural produce rose by 18 per cent between 1900 and 1913.

No doubt this period of unrest caused some of the problems establishing Monmouth Golf Club. The Club was formed on 25 June 1896 at a meeting held in the Kings Head Hotel, Monmouth. Although the Club was formed mainly by army personnel from a garrison in the area, it was open for local landowners and business professionals to take part.

In its early years Monmouth Golf Club moved around a bit. The first site was Priory Farm. Then the Club moved to Vauxhall, taking over the existing Vauxhall Golf Club. In 1903 the Club moved to Hendre Estate, then in 1905 to Troy Farm. The problem seemed the inability to attract and retain members. In those early days the membership of thirty to forty was not enough to cope with the demands of running a Golf Club. There was long grass in the summer months that needed cutting, and greens that needed maintenance. Eventually the Club closed in 1912. In 1920 it re-appeared at its current site at Dixton.

Although the first decades were difficult, since the restoration of the Club at its current site there has been a great deal more stability. The land was leased from a local farmer and with the help of the Club's first Professional, George Waldron, a nine-hole course was laid out. This was officially opened on 1 October 1921. Although minor improvements were made to the course over the next seventy years, the layout has remained fundamentally the same.

In 1992, however, the Club leased more land and a further nine holes were added. Later that same year the new clubhouse was built. The drainage of the course was improved and buggy paths around

Pat Roberts, MBE: county champion, Curtis Cup player, secretary and later president of the Welsh Ladies' Golfing Union

the course were established in the following years. In 2008 the land was purchased by the Club after intense negotiations.

Today the Club owns its own land and buildings and looks like one of the more balanced Golf Clubs in Wales. It seems to have struck a nice balance between the needs of its members and the financial needs of the Club.

The Club has a strong social aspect with a number of charitable and social activities. There is a solid revenue from corporate golfing, and the 500 or so members are free to turn up and play the course with very few restrictions and no booking times. In 2003 the Club appointed a professional secretary, Peter Tully, and the future looks pretty optimistic.

Uncovering the past
For most of its history it was assumed that Monmouth Golf Club was founded in 1921. It was only after an interesting discovery was made in the mid 1990s that this was found not to be the case. The then President, Ken Brown, was researching the Club's history for the upcoming seventy-fifth anniversary and discovered some boxes of papers in a cupboard in a ramshackle old shed. Amongst the documents Ken found the plinth of a trophy dating from 1896. This led him to make further researches amongst the documents and at the local library. Eventually he discovered the true origins of the Club and the seventy-fifth anniversary preparations turned into the centenary preparations.

Becky Morgan
Becky Morgan, the Welsh professional golfer, was born in Abergavenny and is a member at Monmouth. She plays on the American Ladies Professional Golf Association tour and the Ladies' European Tour. In her amateur days she was a member of the Great Britain and Ireland Curtis Cup teams

of 1998 and 2000 and runner-up at the British Amateur Championship in 1997.

Becky turned professional in August 2000 and qualified for the American and European tours in her first year. She has now had a number of years on the tour. In her time on the tour, so far she has had 16 top ten finishes, 2 top three finishes and 2 top two finishes.

Design of the course

The course is described as undulating parkland. It is set in the Wye valley just north of Monmouth and is a real test of stamina and golf. A number of the holes are up or down hill and the names give a clue to the challenge: 'The Struggle', 'Long Haul', 'Last Gasp', 'Cresta Run'.

It was originally designed by the Professional George Waldron in 1921 as a nine-hole course and has been enhanced over the years with the help of members, principally Phil Harris, Ken Pritchard and Ted Moore, and the local farmer the Club had been leased from, Brian Powell.

The 4 8th hole, 'Cresta Run', is a double dog-leg 450-yard, par 4 that recently featured as number 66 in the book 'Britain's 100 Extraordinary Golf Holes' compiled by Geoff Harvey, Vanessa Strowger. The 2nd hole, 'Cannes Folly' a spectacular 180-yard par 3 with a 150 foot drop, also had a mention.

The players' view

Monmouth Golf Club is 'arguably the most beautiful course in Wales.'

— Monmouth Golf Club promotional leaflet

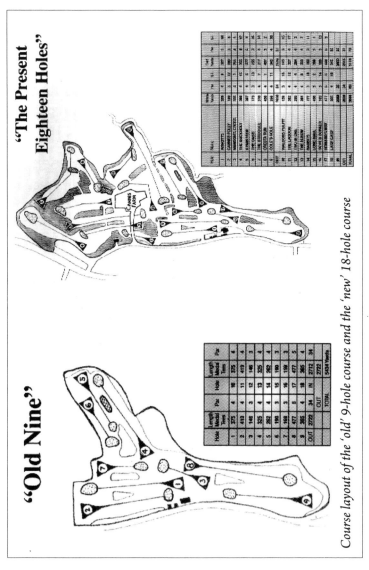

Course layout of the 'old' 9-hole course and the 'new' 18-hole course

'It is a cleverly designed course with plenty of ups, downs, dog-legs, elevated greens, well-positioned sand traps and little ponds.'

– Darren Moseley, *www.golfeurope.com*

'Monmouth certainly has every justification for its claim to be one of the prettiest courses in Wales and is undoubtedly one that is renowned for the warm welcome offered to its guests. The course stands on high ground above the Town with superb views of the Welsh Hills, Forest of Dean and the Wye Valley.'

– www.visitbritain.com

'As you move away from the clubhouse, you become aware of the tranquillity of the verdant surroundings, mature trees, wild flowers and an abundance of wild life such as deer, pheasant and rabbit in particular. Monmouth Golf Club is very proud of its reputation as one of the friendliest Golf Clubs and you are assured of a warm welcome and assistance from the staff to help make your visit a memorable event.'

– www.mediagolf.co.uk

Details

Monmouth Golf Club
Leasbrook Lane
Monmouth
NP25 3SN

01600 712212

Location: Just off A40 0.5 mile/0.8 km north of Monmouth
Type of course: Parkland
Par: 69
Course yardage: 5,698

website: www.monmouthgolfclub.co.uk

Chapter 4

PWLLHELI
Founded 1900

Pwllheli is a strange place: not quite a seaside resort, despite its best efforts, nor yet a town that exploits its illustrious history. Its principal function is as the area's main market and transport hub, making it refreshingly down to earth.

– The Rough Guide To Wales

Situated in the north-west corner of Wales, Pwllheli is the main town and market centre of the Llŷn peninsula. The town was given its charter by Edward, the Black Prince in 1355.

It was once a thriving fishing port and ship-building centre, but these industries have long declined and tourism has been the main industry in the town for over a century. The town is famous as the place where Plaid Cymru (the Welsh national party) was founded in 1925.

In 1947 a Butlin's holiday camp opened and Pwllheli became a thriving seaside town. This camp survived for fifty years until in 1998 it was rebranded as Haven Park.

Today Pwllheli is experiencing a revival as a centre for sailing and tourism. Apart from the outstanding beauty of the Llŷn pensinsula itself, other attractions nearby are the narrow-gauge railway from Porthmadog to Blaenau Ffestiniog, which passes close to Porthmeirion; Cricieth, with its castle and annual arts festival; and the David Lloyd George museum at Llanystymdwy.

False start
In 1891 a golf course was opened in South Beach, Pwllheli. The Club, South Beach Golf Club had a very short life, however, and by 1893 the land was sold and the Club disappeared. However, the Royal and Ancient were adamant that this was the original Pwllheli Golf Club and the Club was believed for almost a century to have a foundation date of 1891.

Start
Solomon Andrews was a Cardiff businessman, tram and bus operator, entrepreneur and owner of David Evans stores, amongst many other ventures. He was on holiday at Llandudno in 1883 when he spotted an advertisement for a sale of land at Pwllheli. He bought the land and developed it into the West End resort. The resort contained houses, roads, a promenade, a hotel and of course, the golf course.

In 1897 Andrews and his son Francis Emile bought a farm (Talcymerau Uchaf) and land for £4,700. A nine-hole course was designed and the course, known at the time as the West End golf links, was played on from 1898.

On 9 April 1900 the Pwllheli Golf Club was officially formed on the site. Initially there were fifty-four members and each paid a subscription of one guinea. A clubhouse was opened in early 1901 and the Club was up and running. The land began to be developed into an eighteen-hole course in 1907 when more land became free; David Lloyd George, Chancellor of the Exchequer, opened this new course on 1 June 1909. The local newspaper reported glorious weather and a large crowd. Lloyd George was given the freedom of Pwllheli Golf Club for the rest of his life. He commended the Club and played a fourball with Arthur Owen (president), William George and J Breen Turner (captain).

The years of the First World War obviously affected the

Lloyd George driving at the opening ceremony, 1 June 1909. In his speech he remarked, 'You have a beautiful course here. I am a great believer in golf.'

Club; by 1921 there were only 149 members. However the 149 decided to lease new land at Cae'r Plan and expanded the course by over 1,000 yards. In 1922 the Club acquired more land and extended the course to 5500 yards. This extension had a special opening where two Professionals, Arthur Havers from West Lancs, Open Champion at Royal Troon in 1923, and Hugh Roberts, Stoke Poges, were paid 12 guineas and 10 guineas respectively to play.

The Second World War forced the Club to close the second nine holes to allow cows onto the course. However, unlike many courses the rest of the course remained open. Servicemen stationed in the area were allowed to play free.

A new clubhouse was opened in 1961, and in 1963 the Club finally bought the golf course land from the Andrews Company after lengthy negotiations.

A clubhouse extension was built, and was opened on 4 July 1981 by Brian Huggett and Neil Coles. Brian Huggett had had nineteen professional wins in his career, starting in the 1950s and extending into the twenty-first century. He would have had no idea that he would have another ten wins in front of him on the senior tour. Neil Coles also had a remarkable professional career, becoming only the second man (after Sam Snead) to win professional golf tournaments in six different decades. The last of his regular career wins was in 1982 when he won the Sanyo Open. Like

Huggett he went on to have great success on the Senior Tour with eight wins on the European Seniors Tour and four PGA Seniors Championship wins.

The Club has continued to flourish. Today the focus is winter golf. The blend of parkland and links, whilst making a fascinating course, can be difficult to maintain in winter and there are tremendous efforts to play the course all year long. This continuous improvement is a feature of the Club, with members always looking to improve the course. The Club is part of the Cambrian Coast Cluster and is targeting people who would not normally be attracted to golf – women and juniors. There is a strong Junior Section with promising teenage Rhys Tecwyn Jones winning the Club championship on four consecutive occasions.

Caddies
Caddies were a feature of Clubs in the early days and Pwllheli has plenty of documentation to give an understanding of their part in the game. A report in the Club archives from 1917 gives a fascinating insight into the life of caddies. At that time golfers bought a ticket from Jack Bowman, Club Professional, and chose a caddy. The ticket cost a shilling. At the end of the round the ticket was returned to Jack Bowman by the caddie, and they were paid 11d.

By the 1930s the job had changed very little. According to the reminiscences of a former caddy, Charles Jones, there were thirty or so caddies at the Club in the summer. They ranged from young schoolboys to grown men, and a few girls as well. Payment was a little higher by then, ranging from 1s 3d to 2s 6d. There was extra money to earn, however, as Charles Jones remembers: 'Iron heads rusted and the caddies got a bit extra from polishing the club-head with sand and emery cloths.'

Jack Bowman

In 1906 Jack Bowman, an apprentice to Harry Vardon, answered an advertisement for a golf Professional at the Club. Fifty-one years later he retired.

In 1916 he enlisted into the army. The Club paid his wages, which were now £1.5s minus his pay as a soldier. In 1927, when Jack Bowman had served twenty-one years at the Club, he was made an honorary member and had his wage increased to £2 a week.

It took another war for Jack to get another substantial pay rise. He returned from war work at Penrhos in 1946 and was made Secretary/Manager of the Club. His wages went to £4 a week.

Jack retired in 1957 and was presented with a £300 cheque at his home at Brook Lea.

Design of the course

The course has had a number of famous designers. Tom Morris, of Hoylake, designed the nine-hole course that Solomon Andrews bought in 1898. That same year it was recorded that 'Old Tom Morris, who is seventy-seven next

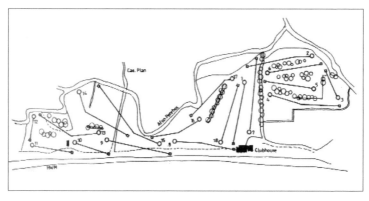

Line drawing plan of course in 1970, showing little
significant change in fifty years

June, has recently returned scores of 87 and 88 at St. Andrews; so that the veteran has evidently not lost the power of his elbow.' (*The Life of Tom Morris*, W. W. Tulloch)

Nine years later, in 1907, another great golfer and golf course designer, James Braid, was hired to extend the course. At this time Braid was at the peak of his career. He had won three Open Championships (1901. 1905, 1906) and would win another two (1908, 1910). Braid designed the additional nine holes on land Solomon Andrews and Son offered to the Club. Although the course was short at 4,690 yards, it was now a full eighteen-hole course.

In 1922 the Club acquired yet more land and extended the course to 5,500 yards. In 1935 another field near Cae'r Plan became available and the course was again enhanced, with the 9th hole replaced and the 10th hole extended.

Throughout its history there has been a philosophy of amendments and enhancements to the course. In the 1950s a number of trees were added. The 1970s saw more changes as new land had become available in 1969. The lake was dug on the 4th hole and changes made to a number of other holes. In 1976 the next stage of course improvements were made. These included lengthening the 12th, 13th and 15th holes, giving the course a length of 5,705 yards.

The players' view

'You have a beautiful course here. I am a great believer in golf. It is a healthy game and a very beneficial game.'

– David Lloyd George (1909),
later Prime Minister (1916–22)

'Located in the market town of Pwllheli on the Llyn peninsula in Gwynedd North Wales. There are superb views of Snowdonia and over Cardigan Bay. The Clubhouse is closer to the sea than any other Golf Clubhouse in the UK.'

– www.walesdirectory.com

'Excellent condition, greens were perfect fast and smooth roll. Some greens felt a little small. Pwllheli Golf Club, very highly recommended.'

– www.reviewcentre.com

'This is a fine course which mixes parkland and links very well to make a good golfing challenge … Enjoy the golf as well as the views and definitely a drink with the locals.'

– Bryn Goodman-Jones, *www.golfeurope.com*

Details

Clwb Golff Pwllheli
Lon Golff
Pwllheli
Gwynedd
LL53 5PS

01758 701644
Location: On coast – signposted from town
Type of course: Parkland/links
Par: 69
Course yardage: 6,109

website: www.pwllheligolfclub.co.uk

View of the eighteenth green and clubhouse, Caerphilly

Timeless Men's Bar at Royal Porthcawl

View of downhill par 3 and clubhouse, Caerphilly

Spectacular view of Caerphilly mountain from the eighth green

View of the short 164 yard, par 3 fourteenth at Newport Golf Club

View of par 4, 426 yard thirteenth at Newport Golf Club

*Third tee with Bristol Channel in the background and
accompanying sheep at Southerndown*

*Breanne Loucks, Wrexham Golf Club junior, now professional,
on the European Ladies tour*

View of the eighteenth green and clubhouse at Southerndown

Driving on the eighteenth at Southerndown

Approaching the eleventh green at Dewstow on the Valley course

View looking west from the fourth green at Llandrindod Wells

View of the stone cottage behind the tenth green at Pwllheli

Hidden gardens at Dewstow

View of Pyle and Kenfig fourteenth green

Approaching the par 3, second at Monmouth

View of Vale of Llangollen Golf Club, clubhouse is to the right of the road at the bottom of the picture

Spectacular view of golfers as they walk along the ninth fairway at the Vale of Llangollen Golf Club

View of course with Llandrindod Wells in the background

View of old farm and church from fifteenth green at Llandrindod Wells

Walking up the seventh fairway at Llandrindod Wells

Spectacular view of Llanymynech golf course

View of the seventh and eighth tee at Rhosgoch

Dewstow Golf Club with Severn Bridge in the background

*View of Dewstow clubhouse and eighteenth green
with the new Severn Bridge in the background*

View of sixteenth fairway from the sixteenth green at Dinas Powys

Dinas Powys clubhouse

Approach to 242 yard, par 4 dog-leg eleventh at Newport

Sir Terry Matthews, owner of the Celtic Manor resort

Fourteenth green at Twenty Ten course at the Celtic Manor resort

Fifteenth green at Twenty Ten course at the Celtic Manor resort

Twenty Ten clubhouse at the Celtic Manor resort

Eighteenth green at Twenty Ten course at the Celtic Manor resort

Chapter 5

NEWPORT
Founded 1903

Ever the poor cousin of Cardiff ... The granting of city status in 2002 was followed a year later by the opening of a Velodrome and an architecturally interesting Theatre and Arts Centre.

David Barnes, *The Companion Guide to Wales*

Newport, the third largest town in Wales, is situated on the south coast of Wales, 20 miles east of Cardiff and not far from the Celtic Manor Resort. Through the centuries the river Usk running through the centre of the town has been a major aspect in the character of the town. At Newport the river has the greatest tidal range of any British river. This has been useful for many centuries as Newport has developed as a port, principally exporting coal and iron in the late nineteenth and early twentieth centuries. However, the unwanted physical effect of this tidal range has been to leave the river a muddy, unsightly looking symbol of the city.

There is a diverse feel about the city. It is a city of contrasts; beauty and ugliness, wealth and poverty, youth and age. It has always been a place of passion, however, and it is no surprise that the Chartists' March of 1839 ended up at the Westgate hotel in the centre of Newport. This march, in protest of a fairer electoral system, ended in bloodshed as twenty people were killed. The Chartist leaders, including John Frost, were later deported to Australia.

The Romans, of course, were in the area betwen 75 and 300 AD, and one of their fortresses can still be seen, together with a National Roman Legion Museum.

Beginnings

Newport is as traditional a Golf Club as you'll get. It has standards. It has values. You know exactly what you'll get at Newport. It's a very traditional members' Club.

It was founded on 7 March 1903, two years after Queen Victoria's death. This was the year Bing Crosby was born, and the first successful flight was made by Wilbur and Orville Wright, in a petrol-engine aeroplane in North Carolina, USA.

Just five months before the official opening of the Club in 1912 the hugely extravagant, corpulent symbol of the previous Edwardian age, the *Titanic*, had sunk with the loss of more than 1,500 lives. The opening came just a few months after the end of a crippling coal strike. It was a year of turmoil as the women's suffragette movement continued its military-style campaign of violence and civil disobedience. There were attempts being made to stave off a war with Germany that appeared to most observers to be

Willie Fernie, Open champion 1883 and designer of Newport course, on the 3rd tee, opening day 1903. Note various styles of headwear!

inevitable. Against this backdrop, perhaps there was a need for some stability, some outlet, some respite for people from this seemingly oppressive period.

The Club began life at Ladyhill Farm and the adjoining Always Farm on the eastern side of Newport. Harry Vardon (six times Open Champion, winner of a record fourteen tournaments in a row) and Willie Fernie (Open Champion 1883 and Professional at Glamorganshire Golf Club) suggested the nine-hole course be extended to eighteen holes, which it was in 1905. In the following years, however, it was acknowledged that there was a problem with the course: the ground was predominantly clay, which was liable to become muddy in winter and hard in summer, so it was decided to look elsewhere for a course which would better meet the needs of the Club.

In 1912 a better place came on the market and the Club moved to its current home at Llwyni Wood, Great Oak on the north of Newport. Llwyni Wood was described as an ancient oak woodland and proved ideal. The Club emblem is an oak tree.

The course was formally opened by Colonel Courtney Morgan, later 2nd Viscount Tredegar on 21 September 1912. In his opening speech the Colonel talked light-heartedly about hunters, who presumably were already in the area, and the new golfers: 'How the hunters and the golfers will get on I do not know. If the hunters rode over the golf greens, the golfers would not be pleased; and if the golfers did not allow the hunters near the golf greens, the hunters would not be pleased.' He then went to the first tee and drove off, whilst the Post Office band played the National Anthem.

By the start of the 1970s the Club was well-established. This was essentially a period of consolidation, although there were signs that the Club was about to face new challenges. It was the great social upheavals of the 1970s, 1980s and 1990s, and the Club's response that caused Dr. Alun Isaacs, author of the *Newport Golf Club Centenary Book*, to describe this period of the Club's history as 'The Re-Awakening Years'. Changes in technology, increased leisure time and social expectations took a while to become incorporated at the Club. However, there was no escaping the conflicts between a new affluent population of people wanting to play golf, and the traditional needs of its members.

The General Committee of Newport Golf Club made a decision that had a fundamental effect on the future direction of the Club. At its essence there was a choice between quality and quantity. On the one hand there was a demand for increasing the membership: on the positive side this would encourage inclusiveness, allow lower fees, more money for course maintenance, etc. On the other hand, this was a threat to the status quo. The quality of service to members would change. More players would inevitably mean more damage to the quality of the playing conditions and result in more players on the course. The committee voted to retain the exclusivity. They voted to limit the membership to 800 from all categories, thereby ensuring the quality of the course and meeting the demands of the members. The path of the Club was set.

Having set a resolute precedent the ensuing decades of social turmoil seem to have had little dramatic effect on the Club. The Club has dealt with change in a practical, pragmatic way. As technology of golf clubs and balls impinged on the course it has been strengthened gradually: bunkers have been repositioned, holes lengthened. Land was carefully bought and sold, and new drainage systems and other changes have been introduced systematically to maintain and improve the course.

Newport sees itself very much as a family Club. Many generations of golfers have played the course. One example is the Davis family, with an unbroken link stretching back to the 1930s and continuing today.

To date twelve Welsh international rugby players have been members of the Golf Club. These include H S Lyne MBE, who was captain of Newport Golf Club in 1905 and 1906, and also President of the Welsh Rugby Union from 1906 to 1947; David Watkins MBE; Stuart Watkins and Keith Jarrett.

Great Oak course layout from the 1930s

Design of the course

In the early years members J. W. Hunt, R. J. Fowler, Garnett Williams and Harold Wood were responsible for many of the designs, changes and refinements of the course. By 1930 it appears that the course was pretty much laid out as it is today.

There have been refinements due to drainage and technological advances, and the course has lengthened gradually from 5,832 yards to 6,472 yards. The par for the course has dropped four shots in this period, from 76 in 1912 to 72 today.

The players' view

'The course is built on a hilltop plateau overlooking Newport and, further north looks toward the valley towns of Pontypool, Risca and Bettws. Southward from the back nine fairways there are views of the Bristol Channel and the Mendip Hills of Somerset.'
                    – Newport Golf Club centenary book

'One of the finest inland courses in Wales. Host to many Amateur and Professional Tournaments.'
                    – www.golfeurope.com

'Without doubt, Newport is one of the pleasantest of the inland parkland golf courses in South Wales, and is surely one of the best layouts.'
                    – www.where2golf.com

'The greens at Newport were velvet.'
                    – Henry Cotton, 1941

'Newport is an 18-hole parkland course that stands 300 feet

above sea level and extends to over 6,500 yards. The course is situated in the magnificent setting of the Llwyni Wood, an ancient oak woodland, surrounded by rolling parkland which contributes to the overall beauty and challenge of the course.'

– www.greensofsouthernwales.com

Details

Newport (Gwent) Golf Club
Great Oak
Rogerstone
Newport.
NP10 9FX

01633 892643

Location: M4 junction 24 to Risca, 1.5 miles/2.4 km
Type of course: parkland
Par: 72
Course yardage: 6,472

website: www.newportgolfclub.org.uk

Chapter 6

LLANDRINDOD WELLS
Founded 1905

Let England boast Bath's crowded springs,
Llandrindod happier Cambria sings.

– The Gentleman's Magazine, 1745
(quoted by David Barnes, *A Companion Guide to Wales*)

Llandrindod Wells, Powys is situated in the heart of Wales. The town is, at first sight, sparse in terms of pubs, but hotel bars more than make up for this. Llandrindod Wells has, at various stages in its history, been a centre for healing waters, the unofficial capital of Wales, and a chic Victorian tourist town. People went there to 'take the waters' for their health, and the local hotels, including the famous Pump House Hotel, were built around this time for the influx of wealthy tourists and their servants. However, it wasn't until the railway reached Llandrindod Wells in 1865 that the town started to really expand. The rail network now connected Llandrindod Wells with visitors from London, Birmingham, Liverpool and Manchester.

In recent years the town has developed as a centre for conferences and functions. This is due to the central location it has from all parts of Wales and middle England. It is this accessibility that led to the boom of the town a century and a half ago, which is replicated every August when the citizens of Llandrindod dress up for Victorian Festival Week.

Beginnings
The Pump House Hotel was the first in the town to
recognise that golf could be an attraction to the area and, of
course, the hotel. In 1889 the owners instructed Alexander
Patrick, Professional of the Royal Wimbledon Golf Club, to
design a nine-hole course. Alexander Patrick had a diversity
of interests. As well as being a golf Professional and golf
course designer he was also part of the second oldest golf
club-making company in the business – preceded by the
McEwans. The course was designed and laid out over the
Common near the lake. For fifteen years or so the game
flourished.

However, in 1905 Llandrindod Wells Council took over
the Common and the number of visitors to the area
increased. The course eventually had to close as it became
increasingly more likely that afternoon strollers would be hit
by golf balls.

However, interest in golf was growing in the town and in
the same year, 1905, Tom Norton, a local car and cycle
dealer, realised what an attraction a golf course would be for
the town. With the help, support and finances of an
architect, two hotel keepers, a medical electrician and two
physicians, he formed the Llandrindod Wells Golf Club
Company. The object of the company was:

> To promote the game of golf and to provide golf links
> and grounds at Llandrindod Wells, together with
> Pavilion, Stables and Conveniences in connection
> therewith and to permit the same to be used by persons
> either gratuitously or for payment.

The company found 140 acres of land on Little Hill and
negotiated a lease with the owner. The tenant at Hall Farm
had grazing rights over the leased land, however, and this

would present a problem that would not be resolved for ninety years.

Harry Vardon (Open Champion 1899, 1903) designed the course and it was playable the following year. A wooden clubhouse was built which lasted almost seventy years.

The company survived for fifty-eight years before a membership buy-out.

Early years

The course was officially opened on 18 May 1907 with a match involving Harry Vardon, J. H. Taylor, George Humble and James Braid. The Club prospered in the early years and a number of improvements were made to the course.

Exhibition matches were popular at the Club, and many of the great players of the day competed. Most memorably, in 1911, four Open Champions played in a match: Harry Vardon, James Braid, J. H. Taylor and Alec (Sandy) Herd.

In 1909 the District Council improved access with a road up to the Club and more land was bought. In 1911 Harry Vardon was invited to design a new course.

In 1914 Sunday golf was allowed with conditions – after 2 p.m. and with no caddies.

In 1918 the Company bought more land and by the early

Eighth Welsh Ladies' Championship, 1912: players and trophies

1920s the Club had two eighteen-hole golf courses, a tea room, an eighteen-hole putting green and a nine-hole pitch and putt course.

Cash crises

When the stock market crashed in New York in October 1929 it had a devastating effect on the world, Wales and Llandrindod Wells. In the years following the crash money was increasingly tight for most people. There was less money to spare on luxuries such as holidays and golf. Many people left Wales to look for work. Some went to America, South Africa and Australia. However, the vast majority moved to England. This pattern was repeated at Llandrindod Wells, an area reliant on two industries: tourism and agriculture. As John Davies writes, 'The 1930s were woeful years for the inhabitants of rural Wales.'

In Llandrindod Wells the Club did what it could to reduce costs; the New Course was reduced to nine holes and the land where the putting course had been was sold. There were problems with staff at the Club, as well as the recession, and competition from a local course. This rival course, Rhydllyndu, had been close to closure but had been saved by the Town Council, and was now a municipal course.

The financial situation had become desperate. Then the Second World War broke out. Llandrindod Wells Golf Club struggled to survive the war. However, early in 1946 a meeting was called to form a new committee and somehow return the Club to its glory days. The Club survived and made steady progress. The members bought the course outright in 1954.Then in 1963 they bought the clubhouse from the Company and a new clubhouse was built in 1973. The problem of sheep on the course was eventually resolved when the Club paid £110,000 and gave the tenant of Hall Farm around 15 acres of land for the grazing rights.

In 2004, with help from the Lottery fund, a driving range was built to provide more revenue for the Club. Like many Clubs Llandrindod Wells is in a similar, if less dramatic, position to the one it was in seventy or so years ago. There is a similar decline in luxuries. Membership is falling slightly, costs are increasing and tourism is declining. The Club members are well aware of the problems and, perhaps strengthened by the knowledge that the Club has survived many ups and downs, are working very hard to solve them. The days of a Club surviving by green fees alone has disappeared. The Club has a Club lottery scheme and is part of the Heart of Wales cluster. There is a great deal of co-operation with Herefordshire Clubs, and the club facilities are being more fully used with the clubhouse holding functions, wedding receptions, parties, etc. A licence has also been applied for which will allow wedding ceremonies to be held at the Club.

The course has held many golfing events over the years. From 1954 to 1961 it was host to the Welsh Boys' Championships and from 2000 onward to the Welsh Golfing Union's Individual Handicap Championship.

The Presidents

Llandrindod Wells has had a number of prestigious Presidents:

- Dr Bowen Davies (1907–1909), the first president, was the first resident GP in Llandrindod Wells.
- Captain F. Phillips was High Sheriff of Radnorshire and awarded the Military Cross in the First World War.
- Field Marshall Earl Haig (1923–26) was Commander-in-chief of the British Army in France. He knew Llandrindod Wells well as he had relatives in the area.
- Lord Tredegar (1927–33) had an estate at Tredegar Park, Newport.

- Lord Sankey (1934–39) was a judge and a Lord Justice of Appeal. He was a member at Royal Porthcawl but was a frequent visitor to Llandrindod Wells, always staying at the Ye Wells Hotel.
- Major David Gibson-Watt (1946–48) was MP for Hereford, Minister of State, Welsh Office, and became Baron Gibson Watt of the Wye in the District of Radnor in 1979.
- Tom Norton (1955), founder of the Golf Club, was made president in 1955 to mark the Club's Golden Anniversary.

Design of the course

The course, high above the town of Llandrindod Wells, has had a tough time over the years. The sheep that were allowed to graze on the land were just one of the problems. The location of the course, above the town is the main challenge.

The course is hilly and was laid out by Harry Vardon in 1905. He was instructed to 'maximise the views from each

Current course layout: 'challenging topology and sweeping views over the lake, the town and surrounding countryside.'

tee and from each green' for the benefit of those golfers who were held up in play. As the editor of *Slow Back: 100 years of golf at Llandrindod Wells* points out, it was more likely that this was added to 'entertain those golfers who had become exhausted by the effort entailed in climbing some of the steeper parts of the course'.

The New Course was also designed by Harry Vardon. A feature of this course was the periscope sited on the 6th tee, which was used to see when the 6th green was clear.

In 1935 the Club asked James Braid to write a report on ways to improve the course. Braid was paid 11 guineas and the actions cited by Braid's report were carried out that year and in subsequent years, when finances permitted.

The players' view

'An 18-hole golf course, established in 1905, features challenging topology and sweeping views over the lake, the town and surrounding countryside.'

– *Slow Back: 100 Years of Golf at Llandrindod Wells*

'The 7th is home to our annual pair of Canada geese. In 2005 this pair raised five offspring and, nesting on a small island in the middle of the pond, managed to escape the attention of foxes but not always of the buzzards.'

– Nigel Edwards (amateur Welsh golfer, captain of Great Britain and Ireland Walker Cup team 2011)

'If you have the time to look to the left as you stand on the tee (16th), you will see the old Welsh church with its graveyard to the side facing the course. Many a silent pair of eyes will be watching you from the graveyard, for many Club members have chosen to be buried there close to their beloved course. They will not pass judgement on a wayward shot because all of them will have done exactly the same at some point in their playing days.'

– Nigel Edwards

'Soon my legs and lungs became accustomed to the task, and I found myself under Vardon's spell. We followed his sheep-mown fairways across the moorland plateau, over ancient stone walls and turf banks to good, true greens, always with a panorama of valleys and far hills.'

– Dale Leatherman (freelance writer specialising in golf)

'Vardon designed a golf course that demonstrates a unique individuality that is seldom seen on parkland golf courses. Vardon's innovative use of the natural environment created a golf course that plays very much like a traditional 'links' course.'

– *www.businessweek.com*

Details

Llandrindod Wells Golf Club
The Clubhouse
Llandrindod Wells
Powys
LD1 5NY

01597 823873

Location: Signposted off A483 at the town
Type of course: Upland links
Par: 69
Course yardage: 5,759

website: www.lwgc.co.uk

Chapter 7

CAERPHILLY
Founded 1905

*Whenever I am asked by people from outside the area where
I come from I always reply, "Caerphilly – it's seven miles from
Cardiff, we have our cheese and the second largest castle in
Europe." Pretty well summed up I think.*

– Heulwen Fowler, BBC website

Caerphilly (*Caerffili*), situated eight miles north of Cardiff,
is the gateway to the Rhymney Valley towns and villages.
Caerphilly was the centre of the Rhymney valleys railway
system that took coal and passengers from the valleys
through Caerphilly to Cardiff. Caerphilly station, with its
four platforms, was one of the busiest in south Wales. In
1901 the railway workshops (or 'the sheds' as they were
known locally) opened, and further cemented Caerphilly's
position as the centre of the rail network in south Wales. In
this age trains were 'the life-line to the outside world from
Caerphilly' and people liked to stay close to the stations.

It seems no surprise, then, that a number of businessmen
and coal entrepreneurs who made their livings in Cardiff
chose to live in Caerphilly. It seems from some accounts
that relatively few of the entrepreneurs and capitalists who
made their money in Cardiff actually lived in Cardiff. Cardiff
was the place they made their money; their lives and homes
were elsewhere. Access to the railway was, therefore,

extremely important to them and Caerphilly, just a short trip from Cardiff, seemed ideal. There were also a number of local businessmen who lived in towns north and south of Caerphilly who were willing to join the Golf Club when it was eventually built, as 'the first tee was within three minutes walk of the railway station'.

From Caerphilly it is not far to Cardiff, Wales' capital city, with the National Assembly building in Cardiff Bay, and a glossy shopping centre. Cardiff has its own castle, and there is also the magical Castell Coch, built in 1870, perched high on a nearby hill.

Beginnings

When Charles Stuart Goodfellow (1867–1952), a solicitor from Caerphilly and Clerk to the Magistrates, was on holiday in Minehead in 1902 he enjoyed playing golf there. On his return he encouraged a number of friends and associates to raise the money to form a Club. A piece of land was leased from a farmer, Jack Lewis of Pencapel farm on Caerphilly mountain, and another plot at an adjoining farm at Plas Watford, and a nine-hole course was developed. It was opened in 1905 with the annual membership fee set at 2 guineas for men, half a guinea for ladies, and a visitor's charge of 1/6d per day.

This was the year Harry Vardon published his book *The Complete Golfer* which had a revolutionary affect on all golfers and introduced the 'Vardon' grip, and the year the dimpled ball was introduced to the game by William Taylor. It was also the year Wales became the first-ever team to defeat New Zealand, when the All Blacks were beaten 3–0 at Cardiff Arms Park in a controversial game that was described as 'the match of the century'.

By 1914 membership had reached 140 and the Club was prospering. However, the war years inevitably brought

Very early photograph of golfers and young caddies at Caerphilly

difficult times for many Clubs, and Caerphilly was no exception. Half the course was taken over for planting food and golf had to stop.

An incident that is legend at the Caerphilly Golf Club concerns a member (allegedly Gower Elias, Club champion seven years in a row (1920–26)). He once landed his aeroplane on the first fairway – there's even a photograph in the clubhouse recording the event.

After the war things returned to normal. However, the effect of trying to restore the Club and the course, and the Depression of the 1930s meant that the Club went through a difficult period of stagnation. The rise and fall of the finances of the Club in this period mirrored the rise and fall of the coal industry. As coal prices dropped in the first decades of the century, so did wages. As the Depression took hold, unemployment in the Welsh valleys was over 40 per cent. There were few other industries to fall back on and the situation was desperate for many. The number of members throughout the period stared to drop. The knock-on effects of the 1926 General Strike dragged on and on: in

September 1929 the minutes record that a sub-committee appointed to arrange a celebration of the twenty-first anniversary of the Club had decided that a mixed foursomes, dinner and dance would be held 'as soon after the General strike of 1926 was settled'. There were just sixty-three lady members and sixty gentlemen members at this time. By 1936 the number of members had dropped to under 100.

The position of lady members at Caerphilly Golf Club would be echoed across many Clubs in Wales. A typical minute of the time has been captured by David R. Brown and Peter T. C. Richards in their well-researched and fascinating book *Caerphilly Golf Club 1905–2005* in the section concerning lady members:

> In April 1937 the ladies' committee asked that their captain and secretary attend Executive Committee meetings. It was pointed out that the rules of the Club do not permit this.

Somehow the Club survived. After another difficult time during the Second World War things picked up as golf became popular in Caerphilly in the 1950s and 1960s. There was a substantial increase in new members and finances. In the late 1950s the Caerphilly Golf Club (Property) Co Ltd finally bought the freehold rights to both Pencapel Farm and the Plas Watford land, with money raised by the members of the Club. This proved a sound investment as the game become more and more popular and those members were repaid in full a few years later.

Caerphilly golf and rugby go hand in hand. The Rugby Club was founded in 1887 and is situated less than a mile (1.6 km) from the Golf Club. Most golf members are keen rugby enthusiasts and often play both sports at a variety of levels. A handful of members achieved representational honours; Terry Cook played for Wales at both codes (Union and League), Andrew Moore played for Wales in the 1990s and Alun Lewis achieved the rare distinction of representing the British Lions but not his country.

Clubhouse

As with most Clubs the 'nineteenth' is a large and fundamental element of the whole Club.

Initially there was no clubhouse, and the Club used the farmhouse of Mr and Mrs Lewis, the farmer and his wife who lived next door. In 1913 the Club rented 'Tŷ Mynydd', 28 Mountain Road, a local house, for meetings. In 1938 they built a tin shanty hut with corrugated roof, affectionately known as the 'Pavilion' – and finally in 1972 the new clubhouse was opened.

Controversy

One of the key controversial events of the Club's history occurred in the early 1930s. At this time the Club was allowed to play golf on Sundays and was allowed to sell alcoholic drinks. The problem was the position of the church. Before the 1930s it would have been unimaginable for these decisions to be made. However, religion had suffered a great deal during the depression, especially the Independent chapel: by the late 1930s half the Independent chapels in Wales were without pastors as the debts mounted and mounted. The chapel, still a focal point in the life of many towns, villages was beginning to lose its power. People were beginning to question the unwritten rules of the Sabbath.

This was the background against which the crucial decision of Sunday golf and serving of alcohol was made; in the views of many, chapel attendance, and observance of the

Sabbath, was being further threatened.

In February 1931 a postal vote went to members (gentlemen only). Thirty voted for Sunday golf whilst twenty-one voted against. The Free Church Council sent the Secretary a letter protesting. The Reverend E Pryce Evans of Van Road Congregational Church preached that new paganism had been let loose with people playing golf and consuming intoxicants on the Lord's Day.

Of the sixty-five gentlemen members of the Club eleven resigned, as did seven of the fifty-six lady members. However, on 19 April 1932 at the AGM at Clive Arms it was resolved that 'Sunday golf commences forthwith on the terms offered by the Goodrich Estate for a twelve-month trial period'.

Characters

Grenfell Jones (Gren), the great Welsh cartoonist, was a member of the Club. Gren was born in Hengoed, Caerphilly in 1934. He had his first break creating 'Ponty and Pop' in the *South Wales Echo*. He once said he had been given the advice to draw what he knew. He remarked that he knew rugby and the Valleys, so that's what he drew. He continued drawing his iconic images of Welsh life until his death in 2007.

Design of the course

The original nine-hole course was designed by William 'Willie' Fernie, the Professional at the Glamorganshire Golf Club based in Penarth. Willie Fernie was a prolific designer and had a hand in courses at Turnberry, St Andrews, Southerndown and a number of others. Incidentally, an insight into the work of Club Professionals comes from the job description of Willie Fernie, as quoted by Wray Vamplex, 'William Fernie at Glamorganshire had to start at 7 am and remain until the last member had finished playing'.

Fernie originally laid out seven holes on the Pencapel

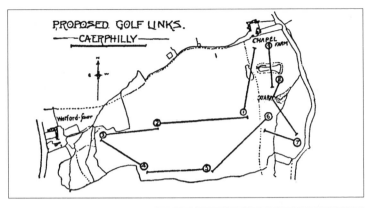

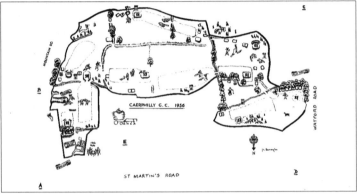

Plan of 9-hole course laid out in 1905, and the course in 1956.
If you look closely you will see a dragon, the quarry,
and drinks at the 19th hole

farm and two holes on Plas Watford. Soon afterward the
whole nine holes were redesigned and laid out on the
Pencapel farm as the Club opened in 1905. There was a path
through the course that became a favourite with locals as
they took weekend walks around Caerphilly mountain.

The course remained substantially the same for almost
sixty years, although by then the path had become the busy
road over the mountain to Cardiff (now the A469), so was
no longer part of the course. In 1963, additional land

became available and three new holes were built. The practice putting green became another hole. With holes 1 to 5 being played twice the course was now being played as an eighteen-hole golf course.

In the late 1980s the Club bought another 45 acres of land. However, due to a variety of problems it was April 2003 before the final five holes were built and Caerphilly became a full eighteen-hole course.

Seventy-fifth anniversary exhibition match
To mark the Club's seventy-fifth anniversary an exhibition match was played on Sunday 9 August 1981. The match was played between Don Jones, Catherine Panton, Pamela Chugg and Brian Huggett. Don Jones was the Professional at Caerphilly at the time.

Catherine Panton was a founding member of the European Tour and won its first order of merit. She won fourteen tournaments on the tour and also played on the LPGA tour; Pamela Chugg also played on the LPGA tour for a number of years and was captain of the Welsh Ladies' team.

Brian Huggett was probably the most well-known Welsh golfer in the 1960s. He had been runner-up in the Open in 1965 behind Peter Thompson at Birkdale. He won the Dutch, Germany and Portugal Opens and had twenty-nine professional wins in his long career. He had also played six times in the GB and Ireland Ryder Cup team and in 1977 captained the team at Royal Lytham and St Anne's, where they lost in the final match before continental Europeans were allowed to compete with GB and Ireland.

The players' view

'The 1st tee is within three minutes walk of the railway station and the little links are generally considered to be most sporting, with plenty of variety.'

– Guide to Caerphilly – 1913

'The course offers visitors a warm welcome and a fine example of parkland golf.'

– www.golfalot.com

'Given that the address of this course is 'Pencapel Mountain Road' you probably won't be surprised that it's a touch on the hilly side. However, don't let that put you off as it is a very rewarding course.'

– www.welshgolfcourses.com

'This friendly members' club offers you the opportunity to enjoy Welsh golf at its best. Caerphilly golf club offers you challenging and exciting golf with panoramic views.'

– www.visitbritain.com

Details

Caerphilly Golf Club
Pencapel
Mountain Road
Caerphilly
CF83 1HJ

029 2086 3441

Location: Three minutes from Caerphilly train station south along Mountain Road (A469)
Type of course: Parkland
Par: 71
Course yardage: 6039

website: www.caerphillygolfclub.com

Chapter 8

SOUTHERNDOWN
Founded 1905

Southerndown is a diffuse holiday village
of touristy pubs and one excellent restaurant.

– The Rough Guide To Wales

Southerndown is a small village on the southern coast of
Wales. It is situated 4 miles south of Bridgend and 2 miles
east of Porthcawl. The village is noted for Dunraven Bay, a
spectacular beach, with its Heritage Coast Centre, and
which has been featured in a number of recent BBC tv
dramas: *Doctor Who, Torchwood* and *Merlin.*

Beginnings
The long, slow changing, unique history of Southerndown
began 360 million years ago. At this time the carboniferous
rock strata was laid down that gives Southerndown its
limestone base. This base is perfect for golf courses and has
phenomenal drainage. Then a mere 12,000 years ago strong
winds blew loess (an acidic soil) over the Ogmore Downs
where it settled on the limestone to create a unique platform
for the tough, grasses that top links courses need.

This natural setting and the natural gorse and bracken gives
the course a unique feel, summed up by former Solheim Cup
captain Mickey Walker: 'I've played golf all over the world
but I've never before played a course like Southerndown.'

In 1904 the exploits of local businessman John Alexander almost single-handedly founded Southerndown Golf Club. He acquired a licence for the land from the Duchy of Lancaster for thirty-one years at a rental cost of £50 per year. £300 was raised initially by eight local business people and the planning and building of the course began in earnest. The original Club was called the Ogmore Down Golfing Society and was registered on 21 August 1905. After a meeting that same month John Moxon, one of the original members, showed the site to a number of potential members, obviously successfully: by the December the Club had raised £3,000 in capital by issuing 600 shares at £5 each. By 1907 they had raised enough money for a clubhouse and the renovation of the course. The Newport architect E. M. Linton, of Linton and Barker, designed the welcoming clubhouse which cost £2,377 to build. This was a staggering amount for the time.

A grand opening

The Club was officially opened on 23 May 1907 when the Earl of Dunraven walked the short distance from Dunraven Castle to the course and hit the first drive. The Club has a feel of nobility and elitism which seems to permeate from land that is now leased from the Queen. The first three presidents of the Club were the 4th, 5th and 6th Earls of Dunraven.

Golf was gaining popularity. However, a report in the *Glamorgan Gazette* from Friday 24 May 1907 gives an interesting insight:

> The cue, the bat, the racquet have taken second place in conversation in places where men most do congregate, and he who cannot pronounce 'golf' with the correct accent is, well, quite out of fashion. Golf is not ever likely

to become the game of the masses, unfortunately.

A further insight into the early years and the attitude of the members has been summed up neatly in the minutes of a meeting in September 1905. Some shopkeepers wanted to form an Artisan Section in September 1906. The minutes record that this would be agreed to, subject to the following conditions:

> That such members have the right to play over the course on Saturdays and Sundays and on any other day, after 5:30 p.m. ... Such members are not to have any right to the use of the pavilion, to take part in the management of the club, to vote at any meetings or take part in any matches or competitions.

In 1909 the Artisans disbanded due to certain members of the Club objecting to sharing the course with local tradesman.

Artisan players at the golf club in 1908. Artisans were elected members of the club, but they were not allowed to use the pavilion, to vote, or to take part in any matches or competitions

The Club was close to extinction after the Second World War. Golf was not very popular: there seemed to be little money to go around. However, as other nearby Clubs closed their members transferred to Southerndown, and somehow the Club survived. Its survival seemed to be due to a mixture of luck and a tremendous sense of commitment by its members. There are stories in the centenary book of the 'elders' of the Club, including Wing Commander Gwyn Williams, who seemed as solid, immovable and entrenched as the limestone base of the course.

For the first ninety years or so the Club carried on, as the vast majority of Golf Clubs in Wales did, in a cloistered world of its own. Change was slow, if it happened at all, and it was usually resisted; any victories were hard won.

The Club was formed in the year suffragettes Christabel Pankhurst and Annie Kenney were imprisoned for assaulting a policeman. Nine decades later, on 1 July 1995, the committee met to decide to give equal rights to women – 'full paying membership'. This was far from unanimous: at the extraordinary meeting – at which only men could vote – the motion was eventually passed by 34 votes to 28.

In the same year the committee made a more radical decision for the future of the Club, which in effect pushed the Club further than any other Golf Club in the area. Private members' Clubs, of which Southerndown was one, had up to that time made decisions through large, enthusiastic, but amateur committees. In 1995 Southerndown gave responsibility for the running of the Club to an Executive Committee of just four.

This impressively radical move flew in the face of nine decades of culture and put the Club ahead of many others. In the fourteen years or so since the decision, it has been the key factor in making Southerndown an outstanding commercial success. The Executive team make hard business decisions. 'The price of a round of golf' has been debated and a modern answer arrived at.

The Chief Executive, Alun Hughes, sees this in twentieth-century terms. The price of a round of golf depends on a number of factors – finance, supply and demand, the needs of the members and the marketability of the Club. Business decisions have been made not to cut costs indiscriminately to compete with other Golf Clubs. The strengths of the Southerndown Club are its history, its exclusivity and its course.

Another change is the Club seeing other courses in the area as occasional business partners, rather than merely 'the competition'. They work with business partners in hotels, travel and leisure and seem to have recognised that golf is changing. Societies, once the icing on the cake for many Clubs, have been on the decline in the past decade. However new markets are opening up; golf tours and golf packages are becoming more popular. Southerndown recognise that they can work with Clubs of a similar attractiveness and pedigree – Pyle and Kenfig, Royal Porthcawl, Ashburnham – to offer customers a package. A recent report to the Welsh Assembly Government recognised its importance and the potential of 'golf clusters'.

The language of Southerndown Golf Club today is of investment, market share, diversity and golf clusters. The traditions of the Club are still strong, but things inevitably change. More change is needed as Golf Clubs throughout Wales have to decide which market they are really in. Is it leisure? Is it business? Is it just a place where people come to meet? In many ways, although Southerndown has a long history and a slow-changing lifestyle, it's now become one of the more astute, radical and forward-looking Clubs in Wales.

Tony Duncan

The prize for the Duncan Putter competition was presented by a great stalwart of the Club and of Welsh golf, Colonel Tony Duncan. The trophy is a putter which belonged to his father, John Duncan, another great Welsh golfer. Tony first arranged and organised this two-day, four-round, amateur stroke-play competition in 1959. His aim was to have a quality stroke-play competition staged in Wales. Over the years this wish has proved absolutely correct.

Players who have entered but not won this competition include Sandy Lyle, Ian Woosnam, Gordon Brand, Philip Parkin and Roger Chapman. Players who have played in the competition and have won include Peter McEvoy, Phil Price, Stephen Dodd, Bradley Dredge, Peter Townsend, Gary Wolstenholme and Jamie Donaldson.

Tony Duncan's other claim to fame, or notoriety, involved a clash with golf legend Jack Nicklaus. In 1966 Tony was referee in the Piccadilly World Golf Championships at Wentworth. After a poor shot Nicklaus asked for relief from an advertising sign under the 'line of sight' rule (i.e. If the referee agrees that the player cannot see the green because a man-made object is in their way, the player may drop the ball away from his line of sight). Tony refused to let him have a drop. Jack Nicklaus was not amused, and when asked if he wanted to change the official he replied, 'I'd like one who knows the rules.' Apparently there were a series of bad natured exchanges between the pair following the championship and they never met or spoke to each other again.

Henry Cotton commented on the decision: 'I wish there were more referees like Tony Duncan – as fair, as knowledgeable and as experienced.'

Design of the course

Willie Fernie, Open winner in 1883, and Professional at the Glamorganshire Golf Club based in Penarth, designed the original course in 1904. Unlike most Golf Clubs the problem seemed to be limiting the course to eighteen holes. A local newspaper wrote that 'no less than 36 perfect ones can be made.' Fernie, who also had a hand in making alterations and designing others courses including the Old Course at St Andrews, Royal Troon and Caerphilly, originally planned a course

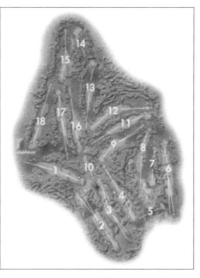

Current course layout. Mickey Walker says, 'I've played golf all over the world but I've never before played a course like Southerndown.'

of 7,110 yards, including seven holes of 500 yards or more. At this time Championship courses averaged around 6,000 yards with St. Andrews being the longest at 6,323 yards. This plan however never came to full fruition as the Committee decided to build a Clubhouse over his design and eventually the course was laid out at 6,900 yards.

The course has had a number of alterations in its history. In 1907 Herbert Fowler made a number of refinements. His main criticism seems to be pretty apparent, as he wrote to his friend Mr. Nicholl, a member: 'At present the great blot on your course is the want of good short holes, in my opinion you have none at all.'

In 1914 Willie Park Junior (son of Open Champion Willie Park Senior, and designer of Sunningdale golf course) was paid 15 guineas plus expenses to visit the course and make suggestions. He recommended some radical changes. These included adding forty new bunkers, and essentially doing away with five holes, with the result that the course would now measure around 6,300 yards. The war intervened, however, and many of the changes, especially the bunker work, were never completed.

In 1919 it was recognised that the course was too difficult. At this time it was said that there was one sand trap for every day of the year on the course. Along with the narrow fairways and gorse this was proving too difficult and too time-consuming (five-hour rounds were common and were unpopular with many members). So, Harry Shapland Colt, the famous architect of over 300 courses throughout the world, including local rivals Royal Porthcawl, was invited to visit the course and advise the Committee. He recommended a number of changes, including reducing the number of sand traps by 200 or so, leaving 126. By March 1920 Colt's recommendations had been completed at a cost of £300.

The players' view

'Overlooking the Ogmore Estuary and Porthcawl, Southerndown is a golf course of great natural feel, with crisp turf, rippling fairways, gorse and bracken everywhere and even sheep for companionship throughout your round!'
– *www.golftravelengland.com*

'Bracken to the left of you, bracken to the right and a fairway rising up to the sky.'
– Henry Cotton

'Southerndown is a hidden gem – a unique course, part sandy links, part acid-heathland. Its unique terrain makes it one of the driest courses in Wales, with year-round golf for members and visitors alike. The course rarely closes.'

– Majid Maher

'It is ideal golfing country with every variety of hole. The turf is as springy as you can desire. You are fairly high up and will receive all the ozone you can cope with whilst the greens are of the finest texture and condition I have found.'

– *Round The South Wales Courses* – Clem Lewis, 1931

'As you glimpse the Southerndown clubhouse in the distance from one of the closing holes, it looks squat and sturdy, indescribable even, completely at one with its surroundings.'

– John Hopkins, *Golf Wales*

Details

Southerndown Golf Club
Ogmore-by-Sea
Bridgend
CF32 0QP

01656 881112

Location: 3 miles/4.8 km from Bridgend on the Ogmore Road
Type of course: Championship downland / links
Par: 70
Course yardage: 6,449

website: www.southerndowngolfclub.co.uk

Chapter 9

WREXHAM
Founded 1906

*Today, in the new millennium I find a clean town of easy
proportion, with a scattering of fine Victorian and Georgian
buildings still extant among the branches of Wallis,
Next and Burton.*

– Peter Finch, *Real Wales*

The town of Wrexham is very solid, safe and dependable. In
some ways it harks back to the era before the industrial
revolution. There were still hints of a feudal system of sorts
in place as late as the mid nineteenth century. 'In 1841 the
town celebrated the fourth Sir Watkin Williams Wynn's
coming of age for three whole days with a procession
through the town and a great feast laid on in the High
Street.'

This was to change as Wrexham's businessmen and
professional people began to gain more power and influence
in the town:

> In 1800 Wrexham was 'a decayed genteel town' of under
> 3000 people. By 1900 it was 'an improved and improving
> commercial centre' of over 15,000 people. It was a
> century of change and the old ways were under pressure.

> Jonathan Gammond, Interpretation Officer,
> Wrexham Museum

Situated close to the eastern border of Wales, and with the closest large towns and cities in England, Wrexham is very much a confused and confusing town. Today there is a sense of industry, modernisation and drive about the area, yet there is still a culture of markets and farming about the place. Even though the change cited by Jonathan Gammond was carried out a century ago, in some areas there does not seem to have been too much progress.

The Bersham Heritage Centre and Ironworks is the place to discover the industrial heritage of Wrexham and the area, while the beautiful eighteenth-century stately home Erddig Hall is amongst other things a memorial to the servants of the time.

The Golf Club

There are echoes of this clash between the old and the new at the Golf Club. The course is a long, well set tradition solid golf course. The clubhouse is 40 years old and feels solid and traditional. The Club has history, it has character and it has its quirks: on the first day of the new golf season (the captain's drive-in day) there is a ritual of firing a shotgun on the captain's backswing.

Eric Room's book of the first seventy-five years of the Club, *Wrexham Golf Club – Its History Since 1906*, tells of the founding of the Club and gives an interesting perspective: 'It was from the ranks of professional and business people that the Club membership was chiefly drawn. It was a compact Club and easily sustainable financially by the existing membership.'

In discussion with Richard West, Secretary/Manager, it was evident that the Club values its excellent reputation immensely. The Club is in some respects pleasantly old-fashioned. The members are the driving force of the Club, it's very much a members' Club. The balance between members' interest and finance will be made, but it will be the needs of the members that are paramount. Richard came from a banking and financial background and is using his experience to ensure the balance stays right.

The Club has an active social life. The calendar is very full with quiz nights, cheese and wine events and dances. There are a number of social functions carried out regularly at the Club including a great involvement in charity work. This has been a strong tradition at the Club and the tradition continues.

Even though this is a difficult time for the Club in view of the global economic situation, the Club seems to be well-equipped for the future. The membership is over 1,000 and the Club has taken a number of initiatives including clustering (partnering with other Golf Clubs and businesses) in the north-western borderlands. The future looks promising, although there will be the inevitable challenges.

Beginnings

On 14 March 1906 Wrexham Golf Club was officially formed. The Club leased Stansty Park for seven years to build a course and then in 1912 the 250 members raised £3,500 to buy the nine-hole course outright.

As with many Clubs there were debates about Sunday golf. One of the earliest surviving records of the Club details a fierce debate at the 1908 AGM where Sunday golf was rejected by a large majority.

In 1923 the Club negotiated a 99-year lease with Lord Kenyon at £310 per year at the present location, Borras.

The Second World War brought great disruption to the Club, as it did to many golf courses in Wales. The course was overrun with all manner of machinery to prevent enemy aircraft landing and an RAF base built on the course, which

Mixed competition photo at Stansty Park, August 1914, a few days before the outbreak of the First World War

was known locally as Borras Airfield. After the war the Air Ministry paid the Club £9,500 compensation and the Club rebuilt the course. This was completed and officially opened on 21 October 1950.

The Club's membership and finances built up gradually over the next twenty years or so, with the course attracting a number of international golfers for a variety of charity and exhibition matches. Amongst the players who played at the time were Peter Allis, Max Faulkner, Brian Huggett, Dai Rees, Christie O'Connor (senior). A new clubhouse was opened in 1968 and the Club has continued to make steady progress ever since.

The Club bought the land at Borras outright for £25,000 in the 1970s with the help of the Welsh Sports Council.

Over the past three decades to the centenary the Club seems to be progressing smoothly and has been able to make amendments to the course, remodernise the clubhouse and stage a number of important amateur events, including the Welsh Club Championship (1991), Ladies' Home Internationals (1995), and the Welsh Ladies' Team Championship (2006).

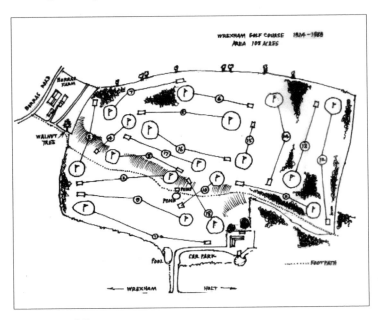

Design of the course

Wrexham Golf Club has had six different courses over the years (the first two courses were played before the club's official formation whilst known as Gresford Golf Club):

> Gresford (nine holes) 1902–1907
> Gwersyllt (nine holes) 1904–1906
> Stansty (nine holes) 1906–1923
> Borras (eighteen holes) 1923–1941
> Borras (nine holes) 1941–1950
> Borras (eighteen holes) 1950– today

Sir Foster Cunliffe provided the first course at BlueBell farm, Gresford, for Gresford Golf Club. However, the Chairman and Managing Director of the United Westminster and Wrexham Collieries, Henry Dennis, believed the area was the perfect place for a colliery. In 1904 he offered the Club a site at Gwersyllt which was accepted. Work started on the new course while golf was still being played on the old course. However, the course proved unsuitable. In 1906 the Bishop of Minevia, the Right Reverend Francis Mostyn, played a large part in negotiating the acquisition of land at Stansty Park from Lady Mary Anne French.

A nine-hole course covering 50 acres was laid out. However, there was no room for expansion and land was found at the present site at Borras. James Braid was commissioned to lay out the new course in 1923. Braid was at the time a Professional at Walton Heath. He won the Open five times and then turned his attention to course design. The construction of the course was carried out and water was laid on at every green at considerable expense.

In 1949 Carter's Tested Seeds Limited won the contract to build the extra nine holes. An extract from their inspection report indicates their approach: 'There are sufficient broken contours, slopes, spinneys, good views and interesting features for holes of character to be designed. The fairways have been placed in sporting and interesting sites. No two fairways and no two greens are alike.'

Juniors

Wrexham has had a very strong tradition for the support of Junior members. As Eric Room points out in *Wrexham Golf Club – Its history since 1906*, 'The oldest surviving item of Club literature is a copy of the Club Rules of 1906 in which is written in a schoolboy's hand, the name of the owner 'Master F. W. Stevens, Junior Member', later to become Club president.'

This interest in juniors from the beginning of the Club's history is unusual for Welsh Clubs formed at this time, but it has obviously paid dividends over the years. Since the 1960s the Club has actively encouraged junior girls as well as boys. It was largely the efforts of Oscar Jones and Ted Clutton that led the way.

There has been a great deal of success, with players Terry Melia, John Wright, Shaun Purdie, Simon Edwards, Matthew Ellis all playing for Wales Boys. Of the girls, Pam Whitley, Karen Davies, Joanne Nicholson, Chloe Williams and Breanne Loucks have all represented Wales.

Today Paul Williams carries on the tradition of coaching juniors with a number of outstanding talents including Breanne Loucks. Breanne made headlines on the Ladies European Tour by gaining her tour card at the age of twenty-one. Breanne was born in Canada but moved to Wales with her family at the age of one. She has been playing golf at Wrexham since she was nine. In a prodigious junior and amateur career she qualified for the Ladies European Tour at the qualifying school on the Costa Calida in January 2009. However, due to a number of difficulties she had to wait five months before making her debut. Breanne has represented Wales and Great Britain and Ireland twice in the Curtis Cup. She made her Ladies European tour at Gerre Losone in the Deutsche Bank Swiss Open in May 2009.

The players' view

'Wrexham Golf Club is situated in the North East of Wales and is considered one of the premier clubs in the area. It offers an attractive, sturdy challenge to even the most gifted of players amid a backdrop of typical, rolling Welsh scenery.'

www.golf.co.uk

'The fact that Wrexham Golf Club is held in such high regard and is unquestionably one of the finest all-round courses in the region is due to the fact that the original choice [of the site] was the right one.'

– Eric Room, *Wrexham Golf Club – Its History Since 1906*

Details

Wrexham Golf Club
Holt Road
Wrexham
LL13 9SB

01978 364268

Location: Off A534 north east of Wrexham
Type of course: parkland
Par: 70
Course yardage: 6,233

website: www.wrexhamgolfclub.co.uk

Chapter 10

VALE OF LLANGOLLEN
Founded 1908

Clasped tightly in the narrow Dee Valley
between the shoulders of the Berwyn and Eglwyseg
mountains, Llangollen is the embodiment of a Welsh
town in both setting and character.

– A Rough Guide to Wales

Llangollen is situated in a perfect strategic position on the River Dee. There has been a bridge on the site for at least 1,500 years and continues to be a place with great access in all directions.

Llangollen ('the church of Collen' in Welsh) was believed to have been named after the sixth-century Saint Collen.

In the eighteenth and nineteenth centuries Thomas Telford transformed the town. Some of the rural charm disappeared with the advent of the Llangollen Canal and the London–Holyhead road. The already tightly-squeezed town was squeezed tighter. Fortunately or unfortunately, the railway link that extended to the town in 1865 sealed the town's fate and it became a tourist boom town.

The opening of the Golf Club in 1908 coincided with the town hosting the National Eisteddfod, which was visited by David Lloyd George and Winston Churchill. It was also the year of the formation of the town football team.

Amazingly the population of Llangollen has diminished over the years. In 1901 the population was 5,704, while latest figures show the population as less than 3,000. This does, however, swell to around 100,000 during the annual International Musical Eisteddfod, which is perhaps what Llangollen is most famous for. This event started in 1947, and sees the town transformed as people from all over the world take part in music and dancing competitions.

Beginnings

The beginnings of the Golf Club at Llangollen are linked with the great tradition of golf and the most famous of all the early golfers, Tom Morris. It was Tom's nephew John (Jack) Morris, then the Professional at Royal Liverpool Golf Club, who came to the area to advise on laying out a course.

In 1908 the Club was founded where it still is – 1 mile (1.6 km) east of the celebrated town of Llangollen, at Llangollen Fechan. The course looks spectacular:

> Nestling on the banks of the River Dee and overlooked by the glorious Welsh hills, this Championship course with its manicured fairways and superb greens attracts golfers from far afield.
>
> *– Today's Golfer*

The original nine-hole course was built and the Club opened at Easter 1908. It was obvious even on the opening day that the golf course was not just for locals. It was also aimed at visitors to the area – especially visitors from a specific area. The report in the *Daily Dispatch* on the laying out and development of the course said: 'This should be good news for Lancashire visitors to the popular Welsh resort, to whom the absence of facilities for playing the Royal game has been a constant matter of regret.' Equally positive reports appeared in the *Daily Mail* and the *Manchester Guardian*.

By the end of the first year the Club already had a membership of 177, a phenomenal effort for the first year of a Golf Club.

In 1910 a clubhouse was built on the old mail route from London to Holyhead (now the A5). The building was large and imposing and cost £276. Internal financial reports from that year reveal that 'ten pounds, seventeen shillings and eight pence was spent on the manures for the course, and horse hire was eleven pounds eighteen shillings and eight pence.' Also the Club hired a coracleman for twelve shillings and six pence – presumably his job was to retrieve golf balls from the river.

With the Club's finances in such a good state the early years were remarkably easy and successful for the Club. Along with the golf there has always been a good social life at the Club. There have been dinner dances, whist drives, fancy dress parties and discos throughout the years, and the clubhouse is still a popular place for local people as well as golf members.

There has always been a large number of open meetings and competitions that encouraged visitors: the Club advertised itself as:

Llangollen and District Golf Club – Attractive Golf Course – River and Mountain Scenery – Commodious Club House, Refreshments, Luncheons, Teas, Motor Park – Open events on all Bank Holidays and Open Summer Meeting.

As the Club developed it was not without one or two minor problems. For instance the sheep on the fairways: A local farmer (Eddie Tŷ Ucha) had his field alongside the Fechan.

*Mrs Platt, Mrs Isabelle Ffoulkes-Jones, Stuart Ffoulkes-Jones and
Tegid Rowlands on the 17th (now 12th) green, 1953*

He was allowed to graze 250 sheep on the course at all times.
However in Open weeks he would waive this right – for a
payment of two bottles of whisky.

The Club continued in its own steady way through the
century. The Club became an eighteen-hole course in
February 1967 when Bryn Dethol Farm was bought for
£40,000. In 1974 a new clubhouse was built and has since
been refurbished and extended.

The future
The Club is proud of its reputation as one of the best in
Wales. In a recent survey it was included in the *Top 100 Golf
Courses* list as a hidden gem. In recent years a number of
National Championships have been held at the course.

According to Bob Hardy, Secretary/Manager, the make-
up of visitors has changed over the years. A great many
visitors still come from the north-west cities of England,
only an hour away. There is more of a diversity nowadays,
and an increase in visitors from all parts of the world, no
doubt helped by the appeal of the town of Llangollen. Golf

seems to have become a worldwide game, and not just a game for a particular class of people. It now seems to be a game for all walks of life and no longer the domain of exclusively professional groups. There is a better mix of young and old, men and women, Bob told me.

The business of running a Club has also changed over the years. Clubs can no longer afford to have an aloof attitude. It is a business. There is a change in the attitude between Clubs. Bob feels that there is more of a 'camaraderie between Clubs'. Vale of Llangollen is involved in partnerships with a number of other businesses and Clubs. There are close links with a number of Golf Clubs in the region, especially Llanymynech (Bob was secretary there), Royal St David's, Aberdyfi, Conwy, and Nefyn and District through 'Golf North Wales' in an effort to offer a regional package to visitors. Vale of Llangollen is one of only a handful of Welsh courses that holds the much sought-after HSBC Gold Medal ranking.

Bob is keen on moving golf further forward. The club believes it should be non-elitist and that the sport itself, the friendships, the respect for others and the honesty should be the pillars that hold it together rather than social class and Edwardian dress codes.

Design of the course

The original nine-hole course at Llangollen Fechan was designed by Sidney Ball of Wrexham Golf Club, with some input from John Morris. The course was an instant success. It was popular with locals and visitors. In its very early years the following comment was received on the course:

> No hedges or long grass, and no cattle or horses on these cleverly constructed and ingenuously bunkered links.
>
> *Centenary Book*

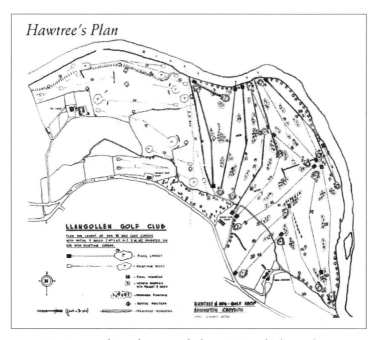

Hawtree and Sons' proposed plan, 1968, which was later amended, much to the annoyance of Mr Hawtree

These original nine holes survive. At this stage there were no sand bunkers, just grass bunkers and long rough to protect the course. In 1968 new land was purchased and the Club started to construct a totally new eighteen-course.

Fredrick George Hawtree, golf architect, designed the new eighteen-hole course. Hawtree and Sons had been designing golf courses since 1912, often working with Open Champion J. H. Taylor. The work began with two Club members, Tom Parry and Alan Jeffreys, taking charge of the construction of the tees and greens, which seems to have been a frustrating experience as decisions were frequently being changed.

When the new course was almost complete there was a change of heart and it was decided that some of the Old

Course holes should be used. The course has undergone a number of changes in the four decades since it was originally built. A variety of options have been tried to help improve the course. The 1st hole, for instance, has been a par 4, a par 3 and is now a par 5. The course is constantly being improved and under review. The 9th hole (the river hole) in particular has been singled out as perhaps the best hole in Wales.

The players' view

'The Vale of Llangollen Golf Course is one of the best inland rounds to be found in North Wales.'
— *www.teeofftimes.co.uk*

'The aptly named 'River Hole' is the 9th and is the signature hole at stroke index 1 on the men's card.'
— *www.welshgolfingholidays.co.uk*

'This spectacular parkland Course is set in the beautiful Dee valley surrounded on several holes by the River. Championship 18 hole course hosting several national championships. Superb greens and fairways. Feature hole is the par 4 9th river hole featured in top holes of Welsh golf. Wonderful finishing four holes.'
— *www.uk-golfguide.com*

'Vale of Llangollen nestles invitingly on the banks of the River Dee and is overlooked by the gloriously majestic Welsh hills. This 18-hole, 6,458-yard (from yellow tees) Championship course's manicured fairways and fantastic greens, combined with its superb reputation, attracts golfers from all over Britain and abroad.'
— *www.northwestgolfandleisure.com*

'Welsh golfers know Llangollen as a beautiful setting for a course where the members of the Vale of Llangollen golf club have played their golf since 1908. The original nine-hole course was doubled in size to a full eighteen-hole course at the end of the 1960s, and the many young trees planted then have, over time, transformed the former farming terrain into a magnificent, modern-day parkland course.'

– www.top100golfcourses.co.uk

Details

Vale of Llangollen Golf Club
The Clubhouse
Llangollen
LL20 7PM

01978 860906

Location: 1 mile/1.6 km west of Llangollen town on the A5
Type of course: parkland
Par: 72
Course yardage: 6,705

website: www.vlgc.co.uk

Chapter 11

DINAS POWYS
Founded 1914

Dinas Powys today still feels more like the fifties than the new century ... The streets are unstraightened, the shops irregular and of a kind now vanished from larger towns – post office, baker, barber – and there are pubs, clusters of them huddled together for drunken warmth.

– Peter Finch, *Real Wales*

The rural village of Dinas Powys, which lies between Cardiff and Barry, had a population of 300–400 until the second half of the nineteenth century. The production and export of coal had a dramatic effect on the village.

From the 1850s the village population increased steadily until the first passenger train arrived in Dinas Powys in 1898. Following this the population expanded dramatically. The rail link turned the sleepy rural village into an early twentieth-century commuter town. The Census of 1901 shows that the village had a population of over 2,000.

A few years later the Cardiff road was built and further increased the population. This small area had become effectively an urban suburb of Cardiff.

The village is not far from the Museum of Welsh Life at St Fagan's, where there is a fascinating and beautifully-equipped collection of period buildings from all parts of Wales, set in 100 acres of parkland.

Setting the timeframe

On 13 April 1914 George Bernard Shaw caused a sensation by using the word 'bloody' in his play 'Pygmalion'. On 8 August Ernest Shackleton left Plymouth on his Trans-Antarctic Expedition. On 27 October 1914 Dylan Thomas was born at 5 Cwmdonkin Drive, Uplands, Swansea.

On 4 August 1914 World War I began.

Beginnings

The residents of Dinas Powys early in the twentieth century were generally affluent and had time on their hands. It was the perfect place to develop a Golf Club. On Friday, 20 September 1912, at The Rise, Highwalls Avenue, six businessmen from Dinas Powys met to discuss forming a Golf Club. The minutes of that meeting and subsequent meetings indicate that although there were only a handful of members at this stage they had a good idea of what they wanted and knew that there would be a great deal of interest in the venture. At that first meeting they agreed that the name of the Club would be Dinas Powys Golf Club; the first fifty members would be known as 'original members' and would pay 1 guinea, with future members to pay 2 guineas; the first fifty women would be known as 'original lady members' and pay half a guinea, while future lady members would pay 1 guinea.

The Club bought and developed 38 acres of farmland from Colonel Gore's Cwrt-yr-Ala estate for £84/6 shillings.

On 27 November 1913 there was a public meeting held with Dinas Powys residents where the members explained their proposals for the land. One of the main issues was Sunday golf. It was agreed that this would be allowed on the condition that there should be no labour employed on Sundays. As a footnote it was agreed that the Professional could please himself what he did on Sunday. This wasn't the end of the matter, however, and the subject came up again at a general meeting of the Golf Club in January of the following year. A vote of 91 to 29 was recorded in favour of Sunday golf.

Other parts of Wales weren't so tolerant. For instance, in Aberdyfi in 1927 Sabbath-breaking golfers were attacked.

Opening

On 2 May 1914, the Golf Club was officially opened. By this time the Club had 200 members (150 men and 50 women) and the land at Highwalls Farm had been turned into a nine-hole golf course.

The day was ideal in terms of the weather and a large number of members turned out to watch the opening ceremony. This ceremony and the first official stroke on the course ('the driving in') was conducted by Joseph Davies, the first Club President. Colonel Gore presented a Challenge Cup, which is still played for.

The first game that day took place between amateurs (C. H. Turnbull, and C. B. Stoddart of Glamorganshire) and R. S. Fernie (Glamorganshire Professional) and the Dinas Powys Club Professional, Harry Prosser. The Committee had decided that the amateurs should be presented with a rack of pipes each whilst the Professionals should be given money, in the form of a 1/- whip round.

As John Hughes, Geoff Thomas, John Bowles and Tom Collins, co-authors of the well researched Souvenir Brochure *Dinas Powys Golf Club, 75th Anniversary* conclude: 'So that was the way the Club began, not with a bang but a whip round.'

Dinas Powys is nowadays a member-owned, friendly Golf Club. It sits in the middle ground of Golf Clubs: it's not a new leisure complex, it's not a hallowed shrine to golf. It's a

Original committee on opening day, 1914 (the president, Joseph Davies, is on the front row, third from left). By this time the club already had 200 members

busy, sociable, fun Golf Club. It is very much a Club that belongs to the members. The officers try to get the balance right for the members. It seems to be a Club where people come to enjoy themselves.

When researching this book I met with the Secretaries, Sally and Roger, and was given access to the records, the history, the clippings, the photos. I was left to dig through original files looking for interesting snippets, minutes of early meetings and press cuttings. There's not too much standing on ceremony for the sake of it at Dinas Powys. It's a Club where people play golf.

Design of the course

In December 1913 a ground committee decided to ask Willie Park Jr., the Mussleborough Professional, twice Open Champion and golf designer, to visit the Club and prepare a report. The cost to the Club was 15 guineas plus his return rail fare.

Harry Prosser from Barry was appointed the Club's first

Professional/Groundsman, and it would seem from the evidence that Harry was the driving force behind the laying-out of the course. He began to lay out the course in January 1914 and within three months it was ready for the grand opening.

In 1921 the additional nine holes were designed by James Braid. Braid was a golf legend at the time. He had won the Open five times between 1901 and 1910. He had started his working life as a joiner in Fife but had moved to London to become a club-maker before becoming a professional golfer. In 1912, Braid became the Club Professional at Walton Heath and became involved in course design. He is regarded as the inventor of the dog-leg.

The players' view
'Everything considered the course was in good condition on Saturday, though the greens, especially after the recent dry weather, were somewhat rough. There is little doubt that when it is more settled it will make one of the pleasantest inland courses in the district, and if extended, one of the best.'
– *The South Wales Daily News*, 4 May 1914

'An undulating course in peaceful surroundings and with a cosy little clubhouse, it is hard to believe it was taken over to the growing of vegetables for the war effort during the Second World War. Now fully recovered, this is a popular place to play, as can be vouched by the membership of some 700, which is amazing in a smallish county that can boast fourteen good golf courses. Worth a visit.'
– *www.touristnetuk.com*

'The course has dramatic views over the Bristol Channel, Penarth and Barry and countryside to the north east.'
– *www.dpgc.co.uk*

'What is it about the Welsh that makes you feel welcome at their golf courses. I found this course by chance, tucked away in the woods behind Dinas Powys, overlooking Cardiff and the bay. Although it is not long, the course has some fascinating holes and the greens were in very good condition. ... You finish with a delightful par 3 in front of the clubhouse where both the meals and beer are all you would expect from a friendly local Club. If you have 3 hours to spare when you are in Cardiff, I cannot think of a more pleasant place to spend them.'

– Peter Clarke, *www.golfeurope.com*

Details

Dinas Powys Golf Club
Old Highwalls
Highwalls Road
Dinas Powys
CF64 4AJ

029 2051 2727

Location: 3 miles/4.8 km south-west of Cardiff off the A4055
Type of course: Parkland
Par: 67
Course yardage: 5,486

website: www.dpgc.co.uk

Chapter 12

TREDEGAR AND RHYMNEY
Founded 1921

When he created the NHS, Bevan said,
'All I am doing is extending to the entire population
of Britain the benefits we had in Tredegar for a
generation or more. We are going to "Tredegar-ise" you'.

Western Mail, 5 March 2008

Rhymney is a typical former mining town, 100 yards wide and 2 miles (3.2 km) long. It's the birthplace of Idris Davies, famed 'angry poet'. Tredegar is slightly bigger: its claim to fame is that it is the birthplace of Aneurin Bevan, founder of the National Health Service. The two towns are separated by a mountain and joined by a road, the A465. It's a place where you're more likely to see a sheep on the road rather than another car. It is situated 24 miles and around a hundred years north of the Celtic Manor golf course in Newport. It's often cold and windy.

The towns are typical, stereotypically almost, valley towns. They are working class, and proud of it. For a long time the towns relied almost totally on two industries, iron and steel, and even though they have all but disappeared a long time ago the scars remain. Since the decline of these industries investment has been episodic, at best. There are a number of green sites in the area and the towns have been improved and redeveloped to some extent. The towns

*Aneurin Bevan, the founder of the National Health Service,
was born in Tredegar in 1897*

probably look better than they have done for 200 years.

Not far away is Blaenafon, with Big Pit nearby – a mining museum run by former miners, with an underground tour. The area is now a World Heritage Site. At 4 Chapel Road, Georgetown, Merthyr Tudful, is Joseph Parry's Cottage. This preserved ironworker's cottage holds an exhibition on the life and works of Parry (1841–1903), most famous for his love song 'Myfanwy' but also the composer of operas, oratorios and many other songs and hymns.

The Golf Club
Tredegar and Rhymney Golf Club is set in Cwmtysswg in the old county of Monmouthshire, now Caerphilly. The golf course is positioned exactly half-way between the coal towns of Tredegar and Rhymney. It's a wild-looking course on the mountain between the Rhymney valley and the Sirhowy valley. It's like going back in time to see how golf courses once were. It's uncomplicated and honest. The clubhouse is an unassuming square building and the people

warm, friendly and welcoming.

The Club is owned by the members and they are incredibly proud of it. Established in 1921, it had a troubled birth, with financial problems from the outset. Coal was the main source of work through the Welsh valleys and this was a time of immense hardship at the very start of the recession. The numbers of miners employed in South Wales pits halved in a few years as the depression hit hard.

In spite of these difficult times there was a determination by the founders of Tredegar and Rhymney to build a golf course. The farm land at Cwmtysswg was bought in 1921, but the first few years proved incredibly difficult and the Club survived only due to the perseverance of a few staunch members. Ironically, at a time when money was incredibly tight due primarily from the rundown of the iron and coal industry it was Mr Tallis, Chairman of the Tredegar Iron and Coal Company, who donated £150 and the clubhouse. This enabled the Club to finally open as a nine-hole course on Saturday 6 June 1925. Dr. E. T. H. Davies, Chairman of the Club, opened the Club with a speech and the opening drive.

The occasion was repeated seventy-eight years later, on Saturday 5 July 2003, when Paul Mayo, PGA touring player 1988–1996, British Amateur Champion and 1987 Open Amateur Medal Winner, repeated the honour when the golf course was officially opened as an eighteen-hole golf course, thanks to hard-working members and, once again, a benevolent supporter: the Lottery fund.

Design of the course

The course was designed and built by Bernard and Cass. The course is perched high on the mountain with spectacular views across both valleys. The holes are relatively short and may seem quite straightforward, on a warm, quiet summer's day. The wind, however, can be bitter

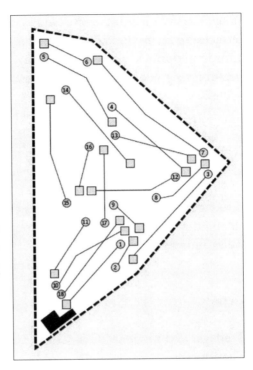

*Course layout:
'Small, tricky greens,
great views,
challenging holes'*

and some of the holes may seem twice as long in the winter. The course is hardy and tightly mown with few trees and relatively little rough. It's very reminiscent of a seaside links course. It's a straightforward course where what you see is what you get. The cost of a round is ridiculously cheap (£15 a round in the summer and £10 in the winter).

The players' view

'Very friendly people. Definitely not one for the silly trouser brigade. Great day of golf. Small tricky greens, great views, challenging holes.'

– A Thomas, *www.uk-golfguide.com*

'The course is a most picturesque one, running in three terraces on the mountain between Tredegar and Rhymney, affording glorious views and the air is heavily laden with health-giving ozone equal to the best spa in England and Wales.'

> – *Tredegar and Rhymney Express*, 13 June 1925

'Very scenic mountain course, lots of hazards.'

> – *www.golfandbooking.com*

'Tredegar and Rhymney is a truly great day out for golfers of all abilities. It is a very tough golf course with magnificent views and very impressive greens.'

> – Matt Glenn, *www.uk-olf-guide.com*

Details

Tredegar and Rhymney Golf Club
Cwmtysswg
Rhymney
NP22 5HA

01685 840743

Location: Take A465, then B4256 between Tredegar and Rhymney
Type of course: mountaintop/links
Par: 67
Course yardage: 5,306

website: www.tandrgc.co.uk

Chapter 13

PYLE AND KENFIG
Founded 1922

*It is rumoured to this day, Kenfig's remains
are guarded closely by a fearsome and deadly Sand Serpent.*

www.visitporthcawl.co.uk

The area of Pyle and Kenfig has had an exciting past. There are myths, legends and stories surrounding the villages and the castle. Kenfig castle really does exist and the castle and the town of Kenfig had a history of being attacked and destroyed for many, many centuries. Today only the ruined stump of the keep is visible.

There are many legends of ghosts and haunted houses across the misty moors and crumbly ruins surrounding the towns.

Today the towns are a great deal more prosaic. They are situated a mile or so from each other and from the M4 and a few miles north of Porthcawl.

There is a huge coastal dune system nearby – the Kenfig National Nature Reserve – with over 6,000 species of birds and flowering plants.

Beginnings
The year the Pyle and Kenfig Golf Club was founded, 1922, was the year of the first Walker Cup Match, the biennial competition between the top amateurs from Great Britain

and Ireland and the United States of America. (Incidentally, the Walker Cup was founded by an American, G. H. Walker, the grandfather and great-grandfather of the American presidents George Bush senior and George W. Bush.)

Just as the time of the Bush presidents was a time of great political and social revolution, so 1922 was a time of great change in the world. This radical period between the wars saw revolution in many places – Russia, Mexico, China, for example – and a number of significant moves away from monarchies to more democratic forms of Government around the world. In the United Kingdom the Lloyd George Liberal-Conservative coalition government came to an end in 1922. In Wales there was the dramatic rise of the Labour Party, and between 1920 and 1922 there were six by-elections in South Wales mining areas, all won by the Labour Party.

In social terms, as well as political and industrial terms, there was unprecedented change. 1922 saw the start of the 'bright young things' generation. In Britain the female revolution was beginning – fashionable skirts ended above the knee, whereas ten years earlier no ankle was shown. Women were finally getting into universities, and learning to fly. It was a radical year for literature, as James Joyce's *Ulysses* and *The Waste Land* by T. S. Eliot were published.

It was a time of great transition and contradiction. The UK was going through a depression yet generally living standards were rising. Steam power was gradually being replaced by electricity. There was a great depression for large parts of the country – especially in the south-east Wales valleys. While for some this was an era of prosperity, it was a period of uncertainty for many and a period of dichotomy for Wales, Europe and the world.

Pyle and Kenfig ('P & K', as it is known by locals) thinks of itself as an artisans' Club. I was assured that it's a Club where everyone can play. I suspect this is a not-so-veiled reproof of its close neighbours, Royal Porthcawl. The Clubs are barely a mile (1.6 km) from each other yet Pyle and Kenfig seems to have been in the shadow of its more prestigious rival for much of its history. 'P & K' seems to be an incredibly well-respected private members' Club, with over 900 members.

In July 1919 Newton Nottage Golf Club was founded and a course established on the sand dunes of Porthcawl. After a year it was decided to disband as for some mysterious reason it had 'become impossible' to carry on. In August 1921 a committee arranged for a lease to construct a golf course on Waun Y Mer common. The course was mapped out by the golf course architect H. S. Colt and opened as Pyle and Kenfig Golf Club in 1922. As a condition of the lease it was stated that 'respectable and reputable persons born and living within the parishes of Pyle and Kenfig and Tythegstone should be submitted to membership for a fee not exceeding two guineas, as long as

Newton Nottage Golf Club team (1921), the nucleus of what later became Pyle and Kenfig Golf Club

the committee approved the application.' This theme of a local Golf Club for local people seems to have been important at the time and still seems important to the 'artisan's Club.'

In *Pyle and Kenfig Golf Club – The First Seventy-Five Years* Colin Wood's excellent research reveals that in the early years 'financial difficulties were never far away from the fledgling Golf Club', yet somehow it survived and prospered.

The minutes and writings about the first years of the Club focus a great deal on the financial difficulties the Club had to endure. For instance, in 1925 the clubhouse caught fire and everything was destroyed. The upshot was a decision to form a limited company and money was raised to build a new clubhouse, which was opened less than a year after the fire. This is just one example amongst many of the resilience and determination shown by the members.

Opening

The nine-hole golf course was opened on 29 July 1922. At the lunch the captain of Royal Porthcawl, Mr T. C. Graham presented 'The Graham Bowl' to the Club. This was first won by E. R. Rowe, and is still contested today. After lunch on the opening day an exhibition match was played between two Welsh Amateur Champions, H. R. Howell of Pennard Golf Club and John Duncan (Royal Porthcawl) versus the Club Professional W. B. Lewis and Percy Allis (Clyne Golf Club Professional and father of TV presenter Peter). Unfortunately the result of this amateur versus professional match isn't known.

The course

Pyle and Kenfig Golf Club's course provides a real challenge for golfers of all ability and with the prevailing winds can turn a relatively sublime mornings golf into an attritional experience when the wind picks up in the afternoon or when the tides are turning.

Colin Wood,
Pyle and Kenfig Golf Club – The First Seventy-Five Years

On losing his ball in the ferns and bracken the experienced P & K golfer will leave his bag on the fairway. There are numerous anecdotes of visiting players finding their ball, but losing their golf bags as they had thrown them down in the rough in order to follow the line of their ball. This seemed particularly true in the 1940s and 1950s when the fairways were narrower and tall ferns grew right to the edge of the fairways. These ferns have been cut back a little over recent years, but the course is still tough and poor shots are punished. Perhaps the character of the course and the character of the Club members have similarities?

The Club has co-hosted the Amateur Championship twice with Royal Porthcawl. The first occasion was in 1988, when Christian Hardin of Sweden took the title. On the other occasion, June 2002, competitors played one round at Pyle and Kenfig and the other at Porthcawl. The top sixty-four players qualified for the matchplay stages at Porthcawl where Alejandro Larrazabal of Spain won the title.

In 2006 the Club staged the Home Internationals which featured top amateurs from Wales, Scotland, Ireland and England. These included Rory McIlroy, Robert Dinwiddie, Ross McGowan and Oliver Wilson.

Design of the course
Just three years after the original nine holes had been established the course was further developed and the second nine added. This course remained unchanged for fourteen years, until June 1939.

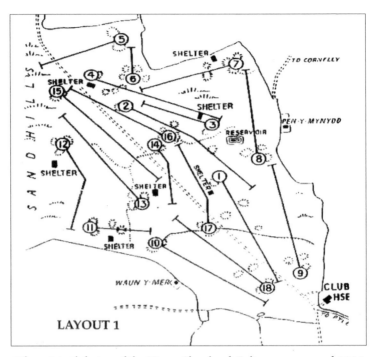

The original design of the Harry Shapland Colt course, around 1925

The original eighteen-hole course was developed by the legendary H. S. Colt. Harry Shapland Colt (1869–1951) became a founder member of the Royal and Ancient Rules of Golf Committee in 1897 and formed the golf architecture firm of Colt, Alison & Morrison Ltd in 1928. The company designed, redesigned and modernised over 300 golf courses in North America, South America, Europe, Australia, Asia, and Africa, including Sunningdale, Lytham, Muirfield, Hoylake, Sandwich and Wentworth Club.

Pyle and Kenfig golf course has two distinct loops of nine holes separated by a road. This road used to be a narrow, rarely-used cart track between Nottage Village and Ton Kenfig. However, in June 1939 Glamorgan County Council widened the path into a metalled road for use during the war.

In 1947 Philip Mackenzie Ross was paid £72 15s 8d to design the current back nine. Mackenzie Ross designed a number of courses including Turnberry. Philip Mackenzie Ross had a philosophy about golf:

> Variety is the spice of life. No two holes and no two greens should ever be alike. Particular attention must be paid to the greens' sites and to their slopes as to the lie of the land on the approaches to these greens. If the course is laid out conforming to these basic principles, then it will prove interesting to all classes of players and will have animation and life.
>
> Quoted in *Golf Course Architecture*

The front nine remains pretty much as Harry Shapland Colt created it. It is more a rolling downland course than a links course. It is fairly short (3,241 yards) and is situated on the eastern side of the road – further from the sea than the back nine. There are a number of challenging bunkers and although this nine has two par 5s is shorter than the back nine. The views are not as spectacular as the sea and sand dunes of the back nine, but it is played over heathland and the greens are usually very quick.

The second nine (3,339 yards) which runs out into the Kenfig dunes and toward the sea, has been designated as an area of special scientific interest, and a European conservation area, due to the presence of rare wild orchids. There are spectacular views of the Welsh mountains, Sker farm, the Bristol Channel and the Gower peninsula.

In 1983 the rare, if not unique, concept of designing six 'A' holes was completed. These were designed principally by P. W. Evans and other Club members to make Pyle and Kenfig, in effect, a 24-hole golf course. These extra holes are used during the winter months to allow a number of holes on the back nine to recover. They also form part of the junior academy and help the Club promote junior golf at the Club.

R. D. Blackmore

Richard Doddridge Blackmore (1825–1900), most famously known as the author of *Lorna Doone*, grew up at Nottage Court, near Porthcawl. It was there that he discovered and later popularised Sker Farm, in his novel *The Maid of Sker*.

The players' view

'The back nine to the west is, well, just mouth-watering, passing through duneland, going close to Sker Farm and the ruins of Sker House.'

– John Hopkins, *Golf Wales*

'Pyle and Kenfig's course closely resembles such famous courses as Hoylake and St Andrews and like these great courses is separated from the sea by a large expanse of duneland. However at Pyle and Kenfig the fairways are more elevated and the course has a greater number of hills and slopes than the more famous championship links.'

– P. Mackenzie Ross

'Pyle and Kenfig, 6,728 yards, par 71 off the back tees, is a course of two distinct halves with the back nine set amongst towering dunes with stunning views of Welsh mountains, the bay and the Bristol Channel.'

– *www.britainsfinest.co.uk*

'The front nine is sturdy, typical downland or moorland turf and played from the back tees on a windy day would present a considerable test. But the run of holes from the 11th to the 16th are sensational.'

– John Hopkins, *Golf Wales*

'However serious the game, time must be made to appreciate the panoramic views. The Bristol Channel, the Gower Peninsula, Sker Farm and the magnificent Welsh Mountains can all be seen from various points.'

– www.golfinternational.com

Pyle and Kenfig, the site of the 2002 British Amateur Championship, has high dunes and deep, disconcerting valleys in a layout that offers plenty of diversity. Two loops of nine holes return you to a cozy clubhouse with the second nine being regarded as the most difficult.'

– Ken Mink, www.travellingadventurer.com

'Pyle's back nine plays over the finest golfing territory anywhere.'

– Paul Williams, www.walesonline.co.uk

Details

Pyle and Kenfig Golf Club
Waun-y-Mer Road
Kenfig
Bridgend
CF33 4PU

01656 771613

Location: 1 mile/1.6 km off J37 of M4 toward Porthcawl
Type of course: Links
Par: 71
Course yardage: 6,728

website: www.pandkgolfclub.co.uk

Chapter 14

LLANYMYNECH
Founded 1933

It Local heroes born in the area:
Richard Roberts, inventor famous for the automation of the
spinning jenny; Ivor Spencer-Thomas, inventor who pioneered
new farming practices during the 1930s depression;
Ian Woosnam, world class golfer, one of the so-called
'big-five' generation in Europe.

– www.absoluteastronomy.com

The village of Llanymynech ('church of the monks') lies 20 miles south of Wrexham and 14 miles west of Shrewsbury. It straddles the border between Powys (Wales) and Shropshire (England). The England–Wales border runs down the middle of the high street, with the eastern half of the village in England and the western half in Wales. When Wales was 'dry' (no alcohol served) on Sundays the Lion pub had a dilemma. The pub had two bars in Shropshire and one in Powys (Montgomeryshire at the time). Customers had to be sure to move to the English bars to have a drink.

The village has had an industrial past with the limestone surrounding the town playing a key rôle. From the eighteenth century it became a large feature of the area. The industrial revolution made the process faster and more efficient as new roads were built linking Llanymynech with Oswestry, Welshpool and Shrewsbury. By the end of the nineteenth century the Hoffmann Kiln was built which further increased the efficiency. With the onset of war in 1914 the kiln closed and the industry in Llanymynech declined rapidly. The restoration of the kiln was the result of a £900,000 Heritage Lottery Fund grant and is the centrepiece of the Heritage Site.

The golf course clubhouse is situated on the limestone plateau at Llanymynech Hill, on the western side of the village.

On the edge of nearby Welshpool is Powis Castle, built by Owain ap Gruffudd ap Gwenwynwyn, and three miles from Montgomery is Dolforwyn castle, built by Llywelyn ap Gruffydd ('Llywelyn the Last') – the last fortress to be built by a Welsh prince in his own land.

Beginnings

The evolution of the course mirrors the economic situation of the time. In the four-year period up to the opening of the Club the Depression was at its worst. In Wales, in this period at the end of the 1920s and start of the 1930s, the producers of wool, mutton, butter, cheese and beef were devastated. As Tim Lambert says in *A Brief History of Wales*, 'Unemployment had already reached 23 per cent of the Welsh workforce in 1927. In the 1930s it grew worse and in parts of Wales half the workforce was unemployed.'

It was during this period that Llanymynech Golf Club came into being. Golf had been played on the course since 1903 when Oswestry Golf Club played on Llanymynech hill. Oswestry continued to play on the site until 1931 when they moved to another location at Aston Park. For two years the course was unused. Then Duncan Wilshaw, Douglas Nicholson, Denny Thomas, Percy Woods and Albert Lowe met at the Cross Guns pub in Pant and decided to put up a guarantee for £400 to form Llanymynech Golf Club and leased the land.

The official opening of the Club was something of a disaster with only Duncan Wilshaw and Tom Owen playing. Despite this setback the first year was encouraging. Membership rose to 145 and a clubhouse, Hill Cottage, was bought. At this time fees were 30 shillings for men and 21 shillings for ladies.

During the Second World War the Club barely survived. The fact that it did so was down to the ingenuity and effort of the members and a reduction in rent by the landlord. At the end of the war the fate of the Club was precarious: the total finances of the Club were down to £70.

Again with a great deal of effort and dedication the Club survived. Then, when the golf boom hit Wales and England in the sixties Llanymynech was in an excellent situation to expand. By May 1971 the Club had an eighteen-hole course with the extra holes having been added gradually over the years. Again this was due to 'hard voluntary work' and 'the initiative, drive and foresight of the then Course Manager, Bob Jones'. The Club survived and flourished over the next decades. In 1996 the course, which had been rented to the Club for over sixty years, was offered for sale for £600,000. It was decided to instigate a bank loan to seize this opportunity and the course, all 160 acres, is now owned by the members.

The Club continues to show the tenacious spirit it has shown over the years. In today's tough financial times the Club has over 700 members, and has been involved in 'clustering initiatives' with Vale of Llangollen Golf Club and Old Padeswood Golf Club amongst others. Club Secretary Howard Jones feels the Club is in a good position. It has a great reputation for friendliness and has a considerable amount of repeat business. The members are proactive and over 160 play regularly in competitions. Howard understands that times are changing and that Golf Clubs need to be run professionally. The skill is to get the balance right. As Howard says, 'It's a members' Club and a business'.

Ian Woosnam

The most famous player at Llanymynech is Ian Woosnam. However, the Club has produced a number of other excellent players, including Phil Parkin, Mark Trow, Andy and Basil Griffiths.

Ian Woosnam as a junior (fourth from left) in 1967

However, it is the Woosnam name that is associated with the Club, and not just Ian: his father, Harold, was captain of the Club in 1973, and his mother Joan was lady captain two years earlier. Ian Woosnam started played golf at the Club from the age of seven at the same time as his friend Alan Lewis, who went on to become green-keeper at the Club. Ian has gone on to play in eight consecutive Ryder Cups, captain Europe in the winning 2006 Ryder Cup and win twenty-nine European Tour tournaments, and of course the US Masters in 1991. The clubs Ian used to win the tournament are not in Augusta, as many of the winners of the green jacket are, they are in Llanymynech. When he was asked why Ian replied, 'Because that's where it all began.' (Incidentally, the Augusta and Llanymynech Golf Clubs were founded in the same year.)

At a very early age Ian had a very competitive side to him. 'I remember seeing Woosie crying in the car because his brother beat him,' said Ivor Morris, a past President at Llanymynech.

Ian's great rival in the early years was Sandy Lyle. Until Ian turned professional Sandy would invariably win their matches. Rather than retreat into himself, Ian was inspired by these setbacks to do better, showing the same tenacity the members at Llanymynech had shown throughout the history of the Club. Ian turned professional when he was seventeen. The first years were tough, and to rub salt into the wound Sandy Lyle had become a European star.

Things improved in 1982 as Ian won his first tournament. By 1991 he had equalled Lyle's feat of winning the Masters and then surpassed him by becoming the No. 1 ranked player in the world for fifty weeks.

Design of the course

The course was a nine-hole course for the first six decades of its life as first Oswestry and then Llanymynech Golf Club played it. However, in an original course layout map dating back to 1914 there is an extra 7th hole. In 1963 extra holes were added and the course became a twelve-hole course. Then in 1968 it was expanded to fifteen holes and finally in 1971 became the eighteen-hole course it is today.

The course is famous for spanning the border of England and Wales. You drive from the Welsh fourth tee onto the English fourth fairway (hopefully). The 4th green, 5th and 6th holes are also in England, then you move back into Wales on the 7th tee.

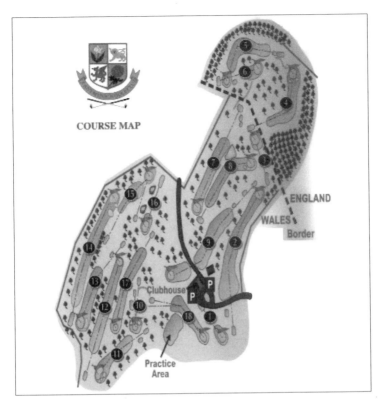

The current course layout, showing the Wales–England border

Another unusual feature is that two of the opening three holes are par 3s.

The players' view

'From the 12th tee the views are just staggering ... Do a full 360 degree sweep from the 12th tee and it is possible to see seven of the shire counties – Flintshire, Denbighshire, Montgomeryshire, Merionethshire, Staffordshire, Cheshire and Shropshire.'

– John Hopkins, *Golf Wales*

'Drive in Wales – Putt in England.'
 – Plaque on 4th hole at Llanymynech Golf Club

'The club itself has the friendliest members I have ever met, and the catering and hospitality are at odds with the stuffiness and snobbery that is often associated with private clubs.'
 – Rob Fitzgerald, *www.golftoday.co.uk*

'This is the best course in the region by some way. The setting is out of this world and the views alone justify the green fees.'
 – GTRBL Golf Society, *www.golfeurope.com*

"I recently played Llanymynech and am glad I did. What a gem. If you love golf try this course. The views are breathtaking, the course very testing, best greens I've played on. Overall I wish I lived closer: I would play every day."
 – Liam Gibney, *www.theinternetgolfclub.com*

Details

Llanymynech Golf Club
Pant
Oswestry
SY10 8LB

01691 830983

Location: Signposted up the hill off A483 at Pant, just north of Llanymynech
Type of course: mountain
Par: 72
Course yardage: 6,047

website: www.llanymynechgolfclub.co.uk

Chapter 15

PENRHOS
Founded 1991

About half-way between Aberystwyth and Aberaeron
is the small village of Llanrhystud, a quiet little place
with a stream burbling down its main street.
On its beach good prawn-fishing can be had at suitable tides.

Ward Lock's *Illustrated Guide Book: Aberystwyth* (1936)

Penrhos Golf and Country Club is on the edge of the village on Llanrhystud in Ceredigion. The village is situated on Cardigan Bay, 10 miles south of Aberystwyth, with its University, Arts Centre, and the National Library of Wales, and 8 miles north of the colourful harbour town of Aberaeron. The National Trust's Llanerchaeron stands just to the east of Aberaeron.

For such a small village (the population in 2001 was just under 1500) Llanrhystud has had an extremely interesting history. The village has encountered a fair number of travellers over the past 1000 years or so. The Vikings were early visitors and destroyed Llanrhystud Church, as well as churches at St. David's, St. Dogmael's and Llanbadarn. A castle, Castell Cadwaladr, was built in 1148 by Cadwaladr ap Gruffydd ap Cynan. It saw a great deal of fighting and bloodshed in its brief history. Two other castles were built: Castell Mawr and Castell Gwarfelin. The narrow ravine separating them is known as Pant-galanas (*vale of slaughter*), which gives some indication of the history of the area.

In the twelfth century the Knights Hospitallers came to Llanrhystud. These close associates of the Knights Templars were committed to good works and caring for the sick. Rhys ap Gruffudd, ruler of the kingdom of Deheubarth in south Wales, gave them the church of Llanrhystud, the village and the Wyre Fach valley. The Knights Hospitallers, after a long and chequered history, still survive in some form as the St John's Ambulance.

Llanrhystud church, which was given to the Knights Hospitallers by Rhys ap Gryffudd in the twelfth century

Since then the village has had a relatively peaceful existence. The main industries in the area have related to farming, although there was a ship-building industry for a while. However, the nineteenth and twentieth centuries were a period of enormous change in farming in Wales. Mechanisation caused a massive decline in employment, and had a devastating effect on the country. In 1951 there were 33,385 farm labourers in Wales; twenty years later there were 11,275. Farms amalgamated as mechanisation made it easier to manage one large farm rather than a number of small farms. Following the Second World War there were 40,000 farms in Wales; by 1971 there were fewer than 2000. The efficiency of farming improved during this period, as did the demand for housing and accommodation for tourists in this area of Wales. Later, farmers faced problems with the European Union as strict quotas were placed on production. All this led to many farms being sold and land being used for purposes other than farming – generally housing, but tourism, leisure and sport were also popular. Welsh land was considerably cheaper than English land and led to 'English colonisation'. Large areas of Wales were transformed as tourism developed as a result of more leisure time and disposable income. This seems to have been echoed in the development of Llanrhystud, and of Penrhos Golf Club.

The Golf Club

Penrhos could be a model for the future of golf. It's a thriving business enterprise set in 150 acres of the Wyre valley on the edge of the small seaside village of Llanrhystud. It is 9 miles/14.4 km from the busy regional centre, Aberystwyth.

In 1966, John and Elspeth Evans of Llanrhystud set aside some of their farmland and developed it into a caravan park for tourists who were then discovering the delights of holidaying in mid-Wales. A decade later there were over 100 mobile homes on site and the family were also running the farming business, with a herd of 120 pedigree Friesian dairy cattle.

As the demand for leisure activities grew the family continued their process of controlled expansion. The golf course opened in 1991, followed by the clubhouse and the leisure centre the following year. By this time the family had given up farming to concentrate on the provision of leisure activities. Rowland Rees-Evans is the Managing Director at Penrhos. His vision for the club is straightforward: 'Our aim is to provide the premier holiday resort facility in the region. This means a golf course that is well maintained as well as challenging, plus leisure facilities that all the family can enjoy and all contained within a beautiful countryside setting.' The business is run by the Rees-Evans family, which consists of three sets of husband and wife teams.

The Penrhos Golf Course and Country Club has tennis courts, a leisure centre, gym, swimming pool, a bowling green, caravans, American style hotel accommodation and an eighteen-hole golf course. It's modern, self-sufficient, and caters for golfers, non-golfers, tourists, locals, individuals and families. The venture works on the same business model used by the upmarket luxury resort at Celtic Manor. It provides leisure facilities, accommodation and golf. The Golf Club has over 200 members with a balanced mixture of men and women, locals and tourists. The clubhouse is a social club where visitors and local people mix. There is none of the sexism you may see at other clubs. There are very few of the conventions of traditional clubs – there are no special times for women, or men, no different areas of the club for members, or non-members.

Rowland Rees-Evans talks about golf and business being interlinked. He has been schooled in business skills as part of the 'Visit Wales' Driving Change training programme. 'Sometimes when you are working in an industry such as golf,' he says, 'you need to see other people's point of view and step back to learn and improve.' Rowland is confident about the future for Penrhos and golf in Wales. More often these days Golf Clubs are co-operating rather than competing, sharing knowledge and best practice. Success – or even survival – these days comes down to basic business principles. 'It's about knowing your market,' Rowland points out. 'Golf today is a business and needs to be run as a business.'

Design of the course
The eighteen-hole course was designed by a local man, Jim Walters, who had had a career as an agronomist, an expert in soil management and field-crop production. The course is set in attractive parkland with plenty of trees and fast, well-maintained greens.

The players' view

'Fantastically scenic with great views of the Wyre Valley, Penrhos Golf course is a great course that makes for an enjoyable round, suitable for players of all abilities.'
– www.teeofftimes.com

'I like to play golf here at Penrhos. With the advent of the Ryder Cup in 2010, hopefully the facilities will allow us to see the next golfing star home grown from this club.'
– Derek Quinnell, on opening the new practice area

'It is one hell of a walk up a very big hill but after 5 holes straight up you will find a flat tight challenging golf course with two superb last two hole to challenge any golfer. The views are brilliant from anywhere. This is a truly rewarding course if you are fit enough to take it on. One of the best in Wales if you can handle the terrain.'
– Gareth Davies, Penrhos visitor

'The climb up to the 5th hole is quite a steep one, but the holes involved along the way are good ones, particularly the dog-leg 4th! But when you get to the top the climb is worthwhile as the views across Cardigan Bay are truly breathtaking.'

– Lewis Rees, Penrhos visitor

'The golf course itself at Penrhos Golf & Country Club is both a good test of golf and an enjoyable round, with a great variation of challenges including elevated tees that exaggerate distances, and strategic ponds set to damage your scorecard. Despite these difficulties, there are some fantastic views from the course, making Penrhos Golf Course one of the most scenic in Wales.'

– *www.teeofftimes.co.uk*

Details

Penrhos Golf Club
Llanrhystud
SY23 5AY

01974 202999

Location: outskirts of Llanrhystud on A487, between Aberystwyth and Aberaeron
Type of course: Parkland
Par: 72
Course yardage: 6,641

website: www.penrhosgolf.co.uk

Chapter 16

RHOSGOCH
Founded 1984

In the community, owned and run by the community,
for the community..

– Rhosgoch Golf Club doctrine

Getting there

On the A470 travelling northward from Brecon towards Builth Wells you take a sharp right turn and pick up the B4594. You climb the narrow road past Llandeilo Graban heading upward into the mountains overlooking the Wye valley. You think you've taken the wrong turning as you pass field after field. You pass small villages: Llanbedr, Painscastle ... seeing more small unmapped roads you're convinced you've taken the wrong turning. Then you turn a corner and see the Rhosgoch Golf and Leisure Club. It seems incongruous having a fully-fledged course virtually in the middle of nowhere.

In fact this golf course is not far from Hay-on-Wye, renowned for its second-hand bookshops, where every spring thousands of visitors from around the world converge for the Hay Literary Festival.

History

This Club was formed in 1984, but the owner went bankrupt in 1998 and sixteen members bought the land.

Since then it has been run as a community members' Club, with the land leased to the members. The members are mainly farmers, some builders, some manual workers, all local.

There is a nine-hole national competition held on the course with the winner going through to the final in Jersey.

Culture

'There is no dress code; all that is required is respect for the course and courtesy to fellow golfers.'

Official website

This Club is unusual. It is another example of the diversity of Clubs in Wales. It's a nine-hole, 2,500 yard golf course. It's a social Club. It's a members' Club. It's the social focus of the community. There are fifty to sixty adult members and about the same number of junior members. On Saturdays children from Rhosgoch primary school play golf at the course. Throughout the summer they have lessons from a visiting Professional and a monthly competition.

There are occasional visitors but not too much passing trade. The Club exists because of the members. The members run the bar, mow the greens, tidy the bunkers, put the flags out.

Talking to Norman Lloyd (Club Secretary, Club Steward, Bartender, anything else that needs doing) about the culture of the Club is fascinating. As you would guess raising money is often a problem – there are 28 acres to look after and people who need paying. The membership fees of £190 must be the cheapest in Wales, and the £12 green fees for eighteen holes for visitors is unlikely to keep the Club going on their own. However, things get done, as they always seem to in a community where everyone has the same aim.

Norman told me that the mower they bought a few months ago involved a bit of a journey as they had bought it off eBay. There are parties catered for, weddings, darts leagues, sixth form leaving parties, the Sunday Carvery, all helping to keep the Club's finances in the black. However, it is the golf that is the focus of the Club. The vast majority of the members play, and seem to play frequently.

Sculptor Peter Michel (left) and Norman Lloyd (club secretary, club steward, bartender, anything else that needs doing . . .)

Character

Peter Michel, retired sculptor and painter, who lives in Colfa, is a member at the Club and has been involved in a number of tasks at the Club (mowing fairways, for instance) and is the Club's official 'artistic consultant'.

Peter has worked on film sets with Hollywood stars at Elstree and Pinewood film studios, making movies such as *Star Wars* and *Indiana Jones and the Temple of Doom*. When he mentioned this to other members he was given the task of designing tee markers. These nine lumps of rugged Radnorshire rock have been transformed by Peter into unique tee markers: 'Every tee should have a proper marker,' he explains, 'and I carved yardage and names on all the stones, among them Heartbreak Hill – it's a long hole and goes up steeply - Shed a Tear (near the shed), Twin Oaks, Amen Corner (a dog-leg corner), and finally, 'Fine Alley'.

Design of the course

The nine-hole course was designed by a local councillor. It's a tight course, well defined and although only 5,000 yards is a real test of skill and precision. 'It's a course for thinkers, not blasters,' I was told.

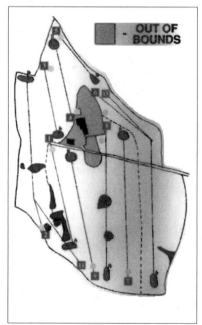

Rhosgoch 9-hole golf course: 'a course for thinkers, not blasters'

The course is set next to a site of Special Scientific Interest – Rhosgoch Bog, one of the few 'quaking bogs'* remaining in Europe. The area supports rare and endangered wildlife and flora. Curlews, peewits, black-headed gulls and red kites are frequently spotted on the course.

The players' view

'Snootiness is not an option at the Club: there is no dress code, the welcome is warm and friendly.'

– *www.rhosgoch-golf.co.uk*

'There are no 'cliques' here – only one big clique, which is nice.'

— Peter Michel, Artistic Consultant

Details
Rhosgoch Golf Club
Builth Wells
Near Hay on Wye
Powys
LD2 3JY

01544 370286

Location: 7 miles/11.2 km along B4594 after A470
Type of course: Nine hole Parkland
Par: 68
Course yardage: 5,000

website: www.rhosgoch-golf.co.uk

* *Quaking bog* or *Schwingmoor* is a form of bog occurring in wetter parts of valley bogs and raised bogs, and sometimes around the edges of acidic lakes where bog is beginning to form. The bog vegetation forms a mat half a metre or so thick, floating over water or very wet peat. Walking on this surface causes it to move – larger movements may cause visible ripples of the surface, or they may even make trees sway.

Chapter 17

DEWSTOW
Founded 1988

Caerwent is now a small village, largely bypassed by the
busy A48 road running between the city of Newport to the
west and Chepstow to the east. It has two pubs, the Coach
and Horses and the Northgate Inn.

– www.wikipedia.org

Caerwent is a tiny unremarkable village 2 miles from the
River Severn and 5 miles east of Chepstow in the bottom
right hand corner of Wales. When the Romans were in the
area in around 75 AD, they built a city, Venrua Silyrum, the
remains of which can still be seen in and around the village.

The site of Dewstow Golf Club takes its name from
Dewi's Stow, the church of St David. Over the years the
manor and estate of Dewstow has passed from a variety of
fascinating families. In 1657 the owner was recorded as
Silvanus Taylour, and subsequently it was owned by
Richard Vaughan Norman (vicar of Magor) and Henry
Oakley (a director at Great Western Railways) amongst
others.

In the 1950s the estate was broken up, with the various
houses and small holdings being sold individually and the
main bulk of the estate being split in two. Dewstow Farm
came into the ownership of W. E. Harris & Son, with
Dewstow House being sold separately. The Harris family

continued to farm the land until August 1988, when Dewstow Golf Club was founded.

Gardens

In 2001, whilst carrying out a general tidy-up of the Dewstow grounds, a workman discovered mysterious pieces of rock. This led to the excavation of the area and gradually a secret underground garden appeared. There had been a garden on the site which contained a number of ponds, water features, rock gardens, tropical glass houses and a vast variety of plants, shrubs and trees from around the world.

There had been stories of a secret garden created by a previous owner, Henry Oakley. As it turned out he had developed both the overground and the underground gardens between 1893 and 1940. His passion was horticulture, and he had employed the firm of James Pulham & Son, landscape gardeners of Buckingham Palace and Sandringham, to help lay out the site. If the above ground garden was interesting, the subterranean garden was spectacular. There were pools and ravines created in a series of tunnels and caverns. There were underground gardens and caves filled with ferneries, plants, ponds and a labyrinth of grottoes and tunnels.

Since their discovery the Harris family have spent £250,000 restoring the seven-acre site and the gardens are fast becoming a major tourist attraction. They have been recognised by the Welsh Assembly Government and granted Grade 1 status.

Beginnings

The 1980s was the decade of Thatcherism in Britain, and the encouragement of entrepreneurialism and small business ventures were key themes of the government. Golf itself was getting more and more popular and it seemed inevitable that there would be a massive boom. Martin Waller of *The Times* wrote about the need for Golf Clubs:

> In the 1980s an industry body asserted that the country needed another 500 courses. There were stories of desperate golfers sleeping in their cars outside the clubhouse to secure a place on the first tee. Some Clubs' membership lists were oversubscribed four, five or six times.'

Dewstow Golf Club was in the right place at the right time and the early years led to expansion of the courses and the facilities.

However, in the past few years a number of Golf Clubs have had real difficulties staying afloat. John Harris, the

Manager, doesn't think any Club can survive by golf alone. 'It is too expensive to run a Golf Club relying solely on members these days. The costs are phenomenal so you need to generate other income.' John is constantly trying new approaches, new ventures to help support the Golf Club. There are cabaret nights, an excellent restaurant, the hidden gardens, comedy nights, quiz nights, etc. It is a hard-working business where the key seems to be diversity and creativity.

This carving by a local craftsman, echoing the totem pole on the Park course, features the golfer's friend – an eagle!

Dewstow Golf Club realise that they're not just in the

Golf Club business. They're in the restaurant, entertainment, leisure time and golf business. Their focus is on doing what it takes to keep the business going through a difficult period. The Club has always been a favourite with golf societies, with two challenging and interesting courses along with the other facilities.

Golf is still the major element of the operation, though, and Dewstow are keen to help popularise the sport in the area. In an innovative idea by Dewstow Golf Professional Steve Truman, the Club will aim to introduce 2,010 children to the sport by the time the Ryder Cup begins on 1 October 2010. The scheme is backed by Ryder Cup Wales, the Sports Council for Wales and Golf Development Wales.

Dewstow is a very modern Welsh golf complex. It has been in a state of continuous evolution over its relatively short lifetime. As with many successful modern businesses it has been flexible and adaptable. The result being that the Club has a healthy outlook in spite of the difficult times for many small businesses in Wales.

Design of the course
Elwyn Harris, with sons John and Mark, opened a driving range and began the process of converting his farmland into a golf course in the mid 1980s. In 1988 the eighteen-hole Valley course was opened. It was built around the natural contours of the estate and thousands of new trees were planted to develop and enhance the course.

In 1993 the Park course was built. This course is slightly flatter and slightly longer. An unusual feature on this course, in the middle of the 15th fairway, is a carved 60 foot Totem Pole, fashioned from a sequoia tree. A local craftsman, Bob Davies, worked on it and designed a symbolic sculpture featuring an albatross, an eagle and other golf-related subjects. Another feature of the course is the 6th hole, a

The par 69 Park course was developed in 1992 and features a number of unusual aspects, including a par-6 hole, and unusual carvings

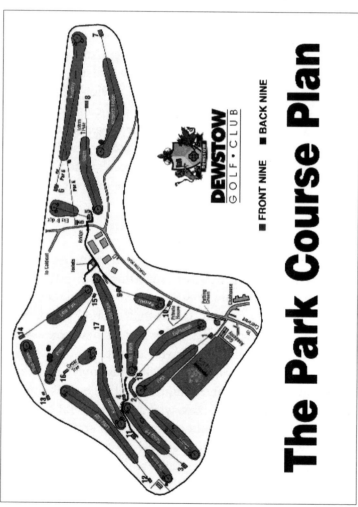

The Park Course Plan

■ FRONT NINE   ■ BACK NINE

monstrous hole which measures 690 yards, and is the only par 6 hole in play in the UK. This course has also been enhanced by the planting of 5,000 new trees.

The players' view

'I recently played the Park course and found it an excellent 18 holes of pleasant, relaxing and undemanding golf. There are a number of pretty holes and half a dozen where you can open your shoulders knowing you could still find your ball in most circumstances.'
– Tony Maplin, *www.golfeurope.com*

'Design of the course is perfect for the mid handicapper with some long par 5s and a good collection of tricky par 4s.'
– Nicholas Maddox, *www.golfmagic.com*

'The Valley course at Dewstow has matured into a very pleasant golfing experience. Most holes have a substantial number of large trees dominating the sides of the fairways. The fairways are well maintained, green and lush and the greens ok; though a touch slow when we played.'
– Ian Thomas, *www.uk-golfguide.com*

'We played the Valley course as a society on the 8 June 2002. Well what can I say. For a short course it is certainly tougher than I thought it would be. Very narrow fairways, tight greens and some very beautiful holes made for a very pleasant afternoon's golf in the sun. I especially liked the par 3 7th hole where you stand about 50 ft above the green with just a narrow gap for you to aim between the trees to get to the green, the green also has water in front of it where several of my fellow players ended up.'
– James Spencer, *www.uk-golfguide.com*

Details

Dewstow Golf Club
Caerwent
NP26 5AH

01291 430444

Location: just off the A48 at Caerwent between Chepstow and Newport
Type of course: parkland
Park course: Par: 72
Course yardage: 6,226
Valley course: par 69
Course yardage: 6,091

website: www.dewstow.com

Chapter 18

CELTIC MANOR RESORT
Founded 1995

Matthews wants to stage the Ryder Cup,
the biennial match between Europe and the US.
'People want to play where the Ryder Cup is played,' he said.
'I have sufficient personal wealth to fund it and I will.'

– Tim Glover, interview with Sir Terry Matthews,
Independent, Sunday 22 November 1998

Back when we started in 2000, bringing The Ryder Cup
to Wales for the first time was a distant dream ...
the 2010 Ryder Cup is now very much a reality
and less than two years away.

Wales Open 2009 Hospitality Brochure
– A message from Sir Terry Matthews

The Celtic Manor Resort is three times the size of Monaco. The 1600-acre site contains a nineteenth-century 69-bedroom 4-star hotel; a 334-bedroom, 32-suite luxury 5-star hotel; two Presidential suites; a 1,500-delegate conference suite; an exhibition hall; forty function rooms; five restaurants; four bars; two health clubs; a shopping centre; two tennis courts; a golf training academy – and three Championship golf courses.

It is geared for the apogee of its existence so far: the 2010 Ryder Cup. It is a phenomenon and has echoes of the great Victorian idealists and entrepreneurs.

Beginnings

The focus of the Celtic Manor Resort is the Manor House, built by Thomas Powell in 1860. Thomas Powell was the largest coal mine owner in south Wales and the biggest coal exporter in the world at the time.

The original Celtic Manor house, built by Thomas Powell in 1860, birthplace of Sir Terry Matthews in 1943, and inspiration for the Celtic Manor resort

The house changed to a hospital and it was here, in 1943, that Terry Matthews was born. Thirty-four years later, the story goes, Sir Terry was driving back from Cardiff to London and saw the old hospital where he was born up for sale. His company, Celtic Inns Ltd purchased the derelict Manor House in 1980. Although there is a tinge of romance in the story, the venture is very much a commercial enterprise. Sir Terry saw the potential in the site and has invested a massive amount of time and money on the project.

Almost thirty years later the resort is complete.

The Resort

In 1888 one of the motives behind the opening of Tenby Golf Club was to attract visitors to the town. Once there they would stay in the hotels, spend money in the town and enjoy the golf. There is obviously an element of that at Celtic Manor Resort. To assume that the whole venture is solely a money-making scheme would be as naive as believing it's a totally philanthropic exercise on the part of Sir Terry Matthews.

Sir Terry Matthews *is* Celtic Manor Resort. At the end of the Victorian age the coal barons of Cardiff and Penarth bought and developed land for their sport. In recent years Sir Terry Matthews has carried out a similar function with his golf resort. The parallels with early Golf Club founders are obvious, but so are parallels with the modern-day moguls, the football Club owners. Terry Matthews has become the charismatic owner and backer of the flagship of golf in Wales. Sir Terry Matthews has become the Roman Abramovich of Welsh golf.

There is a great deal to admire about the way the resort has developed. For instance throughout the development there has been a willingness to share knowledge with other Golf Clubs in Wales.

Jim McKenzie, Director of Golf Courses and Estates Management, is passionate about the amount of good Celtic Manor can do for golf in Wales. Green-keepers visit the Club to look at different techniques, Golf Club Secretaries and Managers visit to network and talk about the future. Jim quoted Einstein's definition of insanity: 'Doing the same thing over and over again and expecting different results'. This was the way some Clubs in Wales behaved. Golf needs to change in order to survive.' He talked about how the £2 million Ryder Cup legacy fund has helped Golf Clubs throughout Wales. It was set up to encourage players new to the game to play golf. There have been projects from

Caernarfon to Carmarthen, and others such as the Driving Change training programme designed to help Club officials become more aware of golf as a business.

'But more than that,' he added, 'there seems to be more of a sense of a Welsh golfing community.' He feels that golf had to become more business-focused. 'Golf alone is never enough to sustain Golf Clubs these days.' Jim's passion is obvious as he talks about the ideal opportunity we have to kick-start golf in Wales on the back of the enthusiasm which will be generated by the Ryder Cup competition. 'Tiger Woods made golf cool. Youngsters have become interested in golf. This is a great chance for golf.'

Unsurprisingly, behind much of the Celtic Manor values and approach is the business philosophy of Matthews. A number of the initiatives are training courses, partnerships, with the emphasis being on working with Golf Clubs, not giving handouts. The quote from Sir Terry Matthews seems to encapsulate this: 'I like things to be profitable and sustained, then they are stable and last a long time. If they are not profitable they will eventually die.'

It's easy to forget that Celtic Manor is a Golf Club. It has several hundred members, monthly competitions and Gareth Edwards as the honorary captain. It's easy to forget because Celtic Manor is primarily a resort. It's a Golf Club but more. It's unlike any Golf Club in Wales. It's impressive. There are estimates that it has cost £200 million to build. It looks like it has. It's cathedral-quiet, non-sexist, non-ageist. As a lady or a junior you can play the same times as the men. It's expensive (£3,000 for a year's Twenty Ten membership in 2009). It's almost too perfect.

Design of the course
The Roman Road championship course was built by the

great innovative golf architect Robert Trent Jones Sr. around the many Roman roads that cross the area. The course hosted the Wales Open in 2005, 2006 and 2007. Robert Trent Jones Sr. designed over 500 golf courses around the World. They include Firestone in Ohio, Spyglass Hill in California and Valderrama in Spain. He was an advocate of golf as a 'no risk, no reward' sport. He died in 2000.

The par 59 academy course for beginners, Coldra Woods, was opened in 1996 and later replaced by The Montgomerie. This was also designed by Robert Trent Jones Sr. and was described by Dale Leatherman as 'one of the finest short courses in Great Britain'.

The Wentwood Hills course was designed by Robert Trent Jones Jr. and opened in 1997. It was built on a difficult area of uneven land and has had a number of changes due to the opening 'ski-slope holes' and difficult climbs.

The Montgomerie opened in 2007 and incorporates elements of the Coldra Woods and Wentwood Hills courses. It was designed by Ryder Cup 2010 captain, Colin Montgomerie. Montgomerie has designed a traditional parkland course that has elements of a links course – deep pot bunkers, for instance.

Under the supervision of architect Ross McMurray of European Golf Design the course for the Ryder Cup is the Twenty Ten course. The course has been specifically constructed for the three-day event, 1–3 October 2010. The course is designed to be exciting, challenging and watchable. There are water hazards on nine of the holes and great visibility for spectators. It's set in a 'big, wide, windy and largely treeless bowl of the Usk Valley'. It's believed that 15,000–20,000 spectators will be able to see the 18th.

Ross McMurray says:'We wanted to create a fantastic stage for the players to walk down.'

The players' view

'If you are a lover of all things traditional, then Celtic Manor is probably not for you. But if you are seeking thrills and an exciting and tough challenge, then Twenty Ten will fit the bill perfectly.'

– Top 100 Golf Courses

'They've done a really good job on the new holes. They have been designed especially for The Ryder Cup and should provide plenty of drama.'

– Ian Woosnam

'The 15th was my favourite. A drive of 250 yards leaves you in prime position and it's a relatively straightforward 130 yard chip to the front of the green. Again, though, an elevated putting surface makes finding the green a priority, drift to the left though, and the water comes into play.'

– Marc Dodd, *Metro*

'The flatter terrain of the 2010 course is home to many excellent holes, accompanied by a multitude of intimidating water hazards and significant bunkering.'

– www.where2golf.com

'The Twenty Ten Course at Celtic Manor was the first course to be built specifically to stage the Ryder Cup, and it doesn't disappoint. The course has no less than six signature holes and numerous risk-and-reward dilemmas to thoroughly test your course planning and golfing skills.'

– www.golf.co.uk

'Great course with one tough memorable hole after another. There's too many great holes to single one out.'

– www.top100golfcourses.co.uk

Details

The Celtic Manor Resort
Coldra Woods
The Usk Valley
Newport
South Wales
NP18 1HQ

01633 413000

2010 Ryder Cup course
Location: M4 exit 24 take A48 toward Newport for ½ mile, or from Newport follow A48 toward Chepstow to Coldra roundabout follow signs to resort
Type of course: Parkland
Par: 71
Course yardage: 7,493

website: www.celtic-manor.com

SOURCES

Clwb Golff Pwllheli – 1900–2000
Dinas Powys Golf Club – 75th Anniversary
Slow Back – 100 Years of Golf at Llandrindod Wells
    1905–2005
Wrexham Golf Club 1906 to 2006 – A Hundred Years of Golf

David R. Brown and Peter T. C. Richards,
    Caerphilly Golf Club 1905–2005
Phil Carradice (ed), *Southerdown Golf Club 1905–2005 –*
    A Century of Memories
Alun Isaac, *Newport Golf Club 1903–2003*
Nev Kynaston, *Llanymynech Golf Club 75th Anniversary*
    1933–2008
J. J. L. Mabe, *Tenby Golf Club – The First Hundred Years*
Leo McMahon, *Royal Porthcawl 1891–1991*
Eric Room, *Wrexham Golf Club – Its History Since 1906*
Ken Williams, *Vale of Llangollen Golf Club – Centenary 2008*
Colin Wood, *Pyle & Kenfig Golf Club – The First Seventy*
    Five Years

Wray Vamplew, 'Successful Workers or Exploited Labor?
Golf Professionals and Professional Golfers in Britain
1888–1914', *Economic History Review 61* (Blackwell
Publishing, 2008)

David Atkinson and Neil Wilson, *Wales*
    (Lonely Planet Publications, 2007)
David Barnes, *The Companion Guide to Wales*
    (Companion Guides, 2005)
John Davies, *A History of Wales* (Penguin, 2007)
Peter Finch, *Real Wales* (Seren, 2008)
Rebecca Ford, *Footprint Wales* (Footprintbooks, 2005)

Geoff Harvey and Vanessa Strowger,
  Britain's 100 Extraordinary Golf Holes
  (Aesculus Press Ltd, 2003)
John Hopkins and T. Werner Laurie, *Golf Wales*
  (Graffeg, 2007).
Robert Kroeger, *The Links of Wales*
  (Heritage Communications, 2002)
Tim Lambert, *A Brief History of Wales*
  (http://www.localhistories.org/wales.html)
Hywel Wyn Owen and Richard Morgan, *Dictionary of the
  Place-Names of Wales* (Gomer Press, 2007)
Mike Parker and Paul Whitfield, *The Rough Guide to Wales*,
  (Rough Guides, 2006)
Graham Roberts, *Around & About – South-West Wales*
  (Logaston Press, 2007)
Mark Rowlinson and Peter Lees, *Golf Courses of North
  Wales* (Ammanford, 1997)
Susy Smith, *Guide to Rural Wales*
  (Travel Publishing Ltd, 2005)
W. W. Tulloch and T. Werner Laurie,
  *The Life of Tom Morris, With glimpses of St Andrews
  and its golfing celebrities* (1908)
David Williams, *About Mid Wales* (Graffeg, 2007)
Welsh Sports Council, *Golfing in Wales* (1999)